MAD
CHEAP SHOTS

AN OUT-OF-FOCUS PHOTO ALBUM BY
PAUL PETER PORGES

WARNER BOOKS

A Warner Communications Company

WARNER BOOKS EDITION

This Warner Books Edition is published by arrangement with
E.C. Publications, Inc.

Warner Books, Inc.,
666 Fifth Avenue,
New York, N.Y. 10103

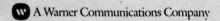

A Warner Communications Company

Printed in the United States of America

First Warner Books Printing: January, 1984

10 9 8 7 6 5 4 3 2 1

INTRODUCTION

The title of this book is "MAD Cheap Shots." It is a book about photography, sort of, a subject I, sort of, happen to know absolutely nothing about.

So, when Paul Peter Porges first approached me about writing an introduction to this book, I immediately began to shutter. "Hold it!" I said. "Any close-up of my credentials would instantly focus-in on my very limited-time exposure to the world of photography."

"Put your negative feelings aside," Porges said. "Take a few shots at it and see what develops!"

Porges was right. I couldn't let my lack of depth in the field stop me. After all, I reasoned, I could always zoom in on some wide angle of photography that lens itself to a glossy enlargement and wind it up in an instant!

So, if you can picture it, I posed myself at my desk in a darkroom and it wasn't very long before things started to click and I was on a roll.

In short, I gave it the old college tri-pod and this introduction was written in a flash!

John Ficarra

CONTENTS

CANDID SNAPSHOTS OF LORES AND LEGENDS

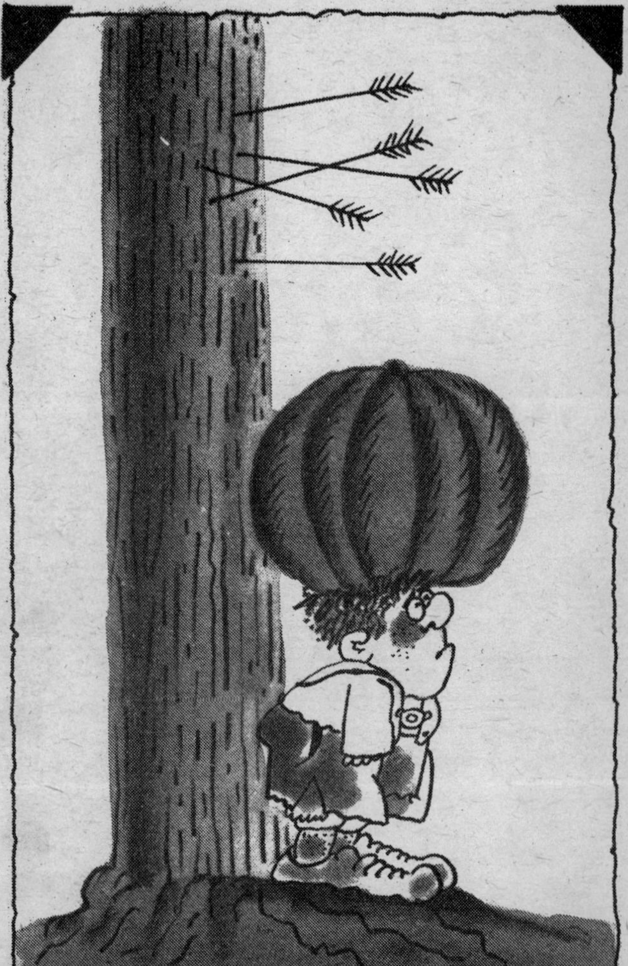

William Tell begins training with a watermelon for an upcoming marksmanship contest.

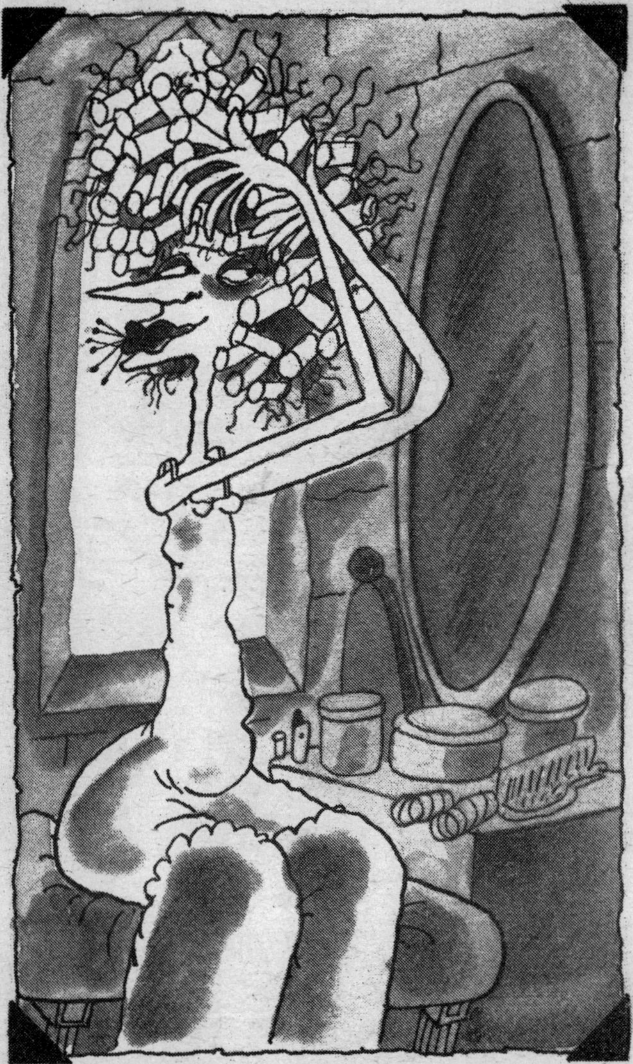

Rapunzel getting ready for a big weekend

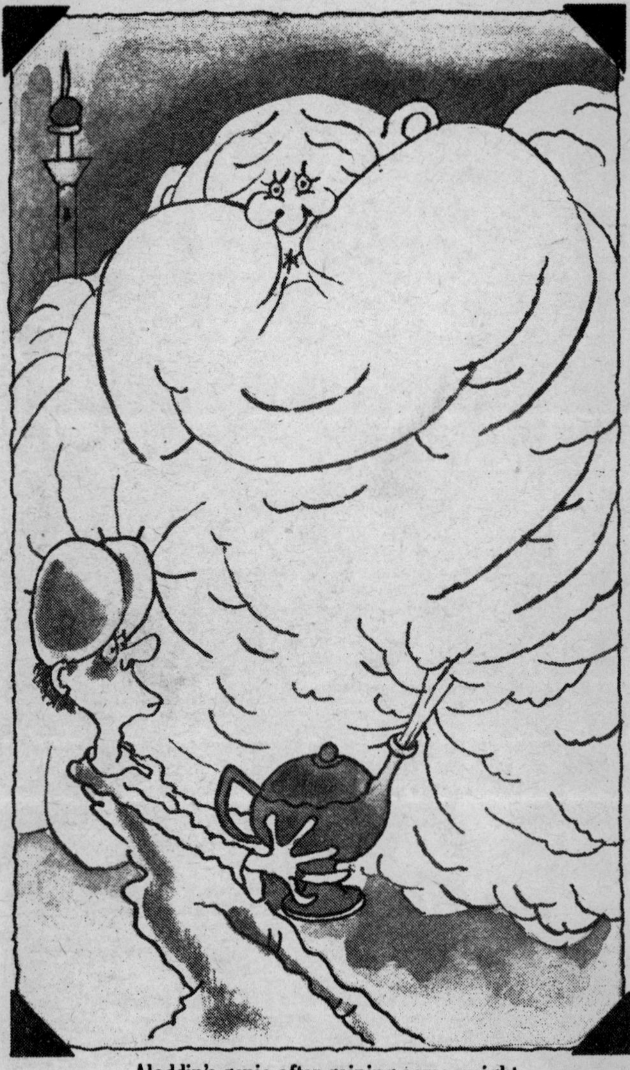

Aladdin's genie after gaining some weight
while outside the magic lamp

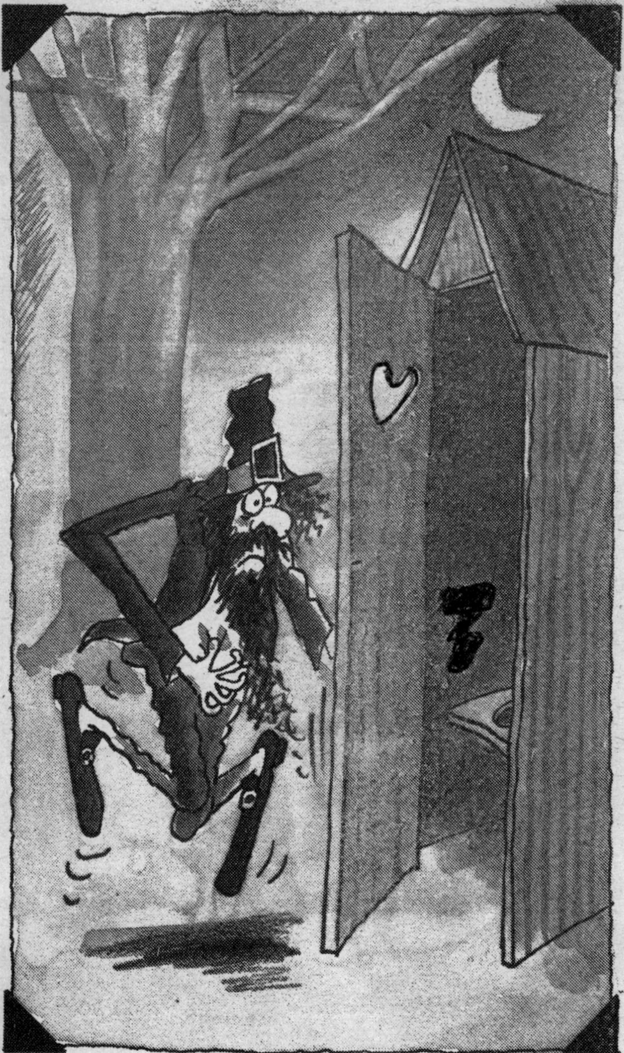

Rip Van Winkle taking a short break
from his 20-year sleep

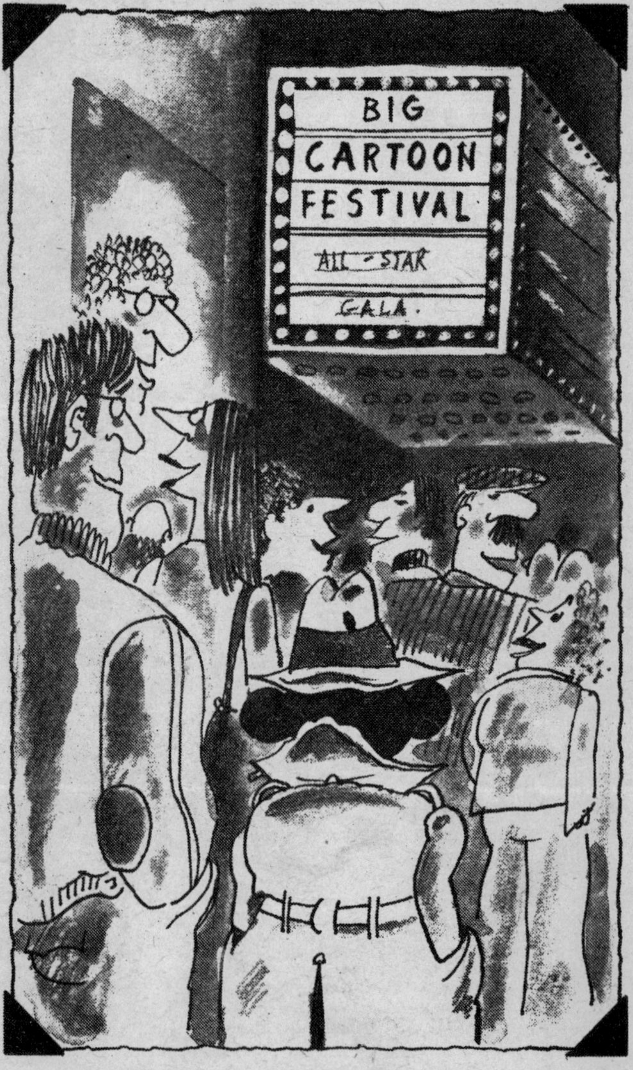
BIG
CARTOON
FESTIVAL
ALL-STAR
GALA.

Mickey Mouse incognito at a Disney cartoon revival

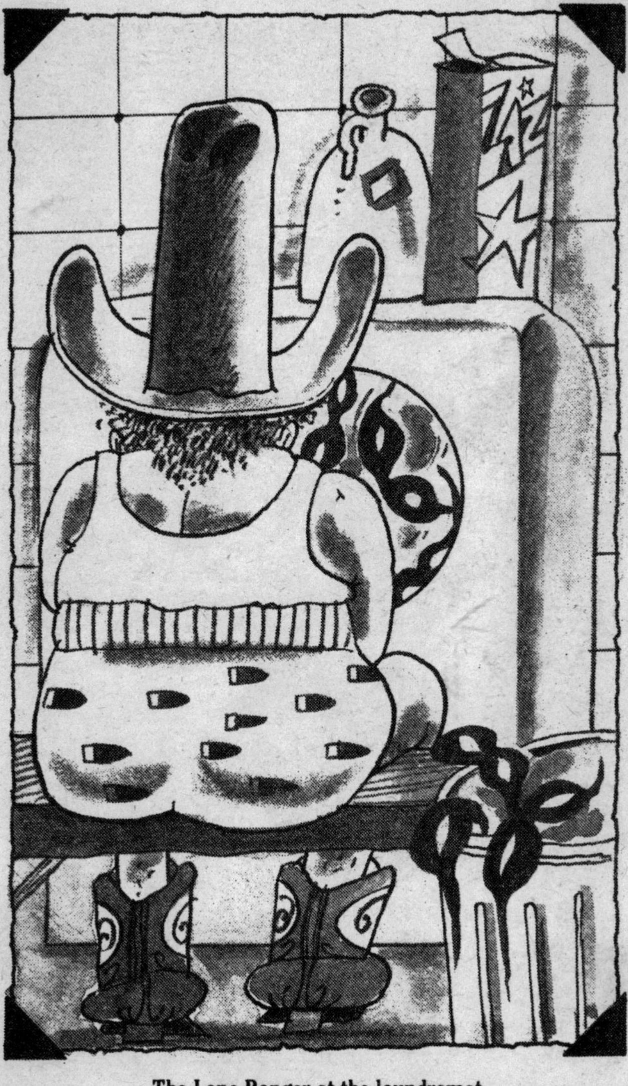

The Lone Ranger at the laundromat

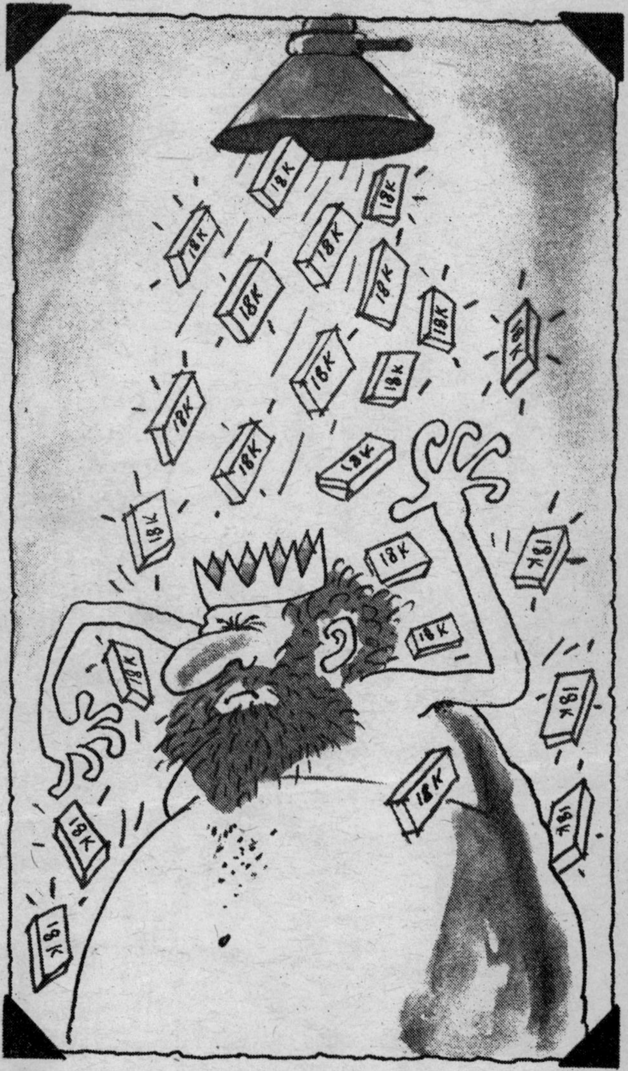
18K

King Midas taking a shower

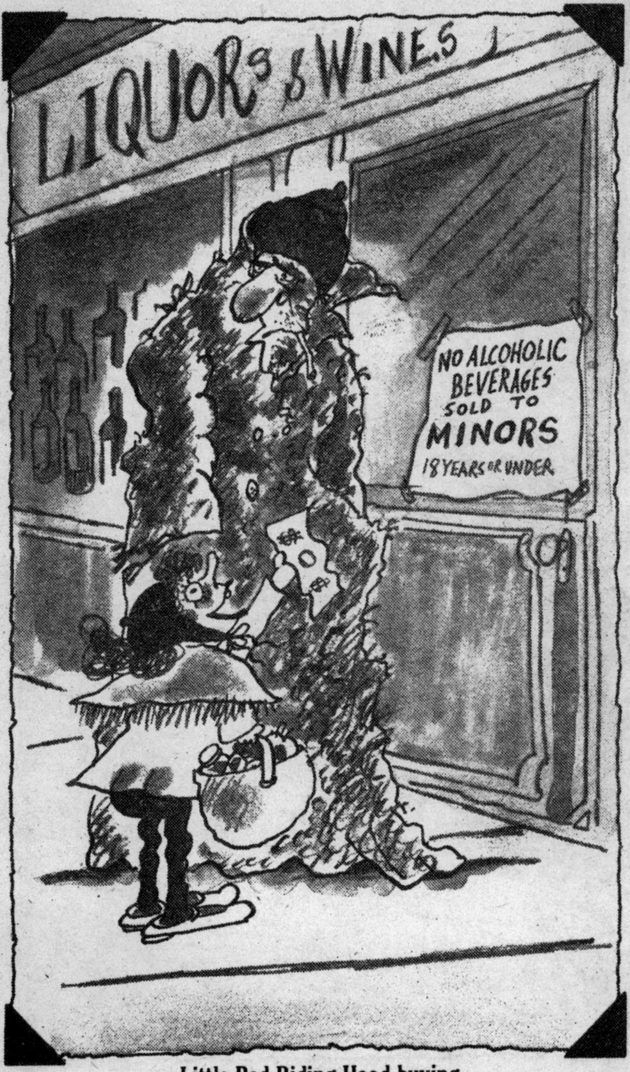
LIQUORS & WINES
NO ALCOHOLIC
BEVERAGES
SOLD TO
MINORS
18 YEARS OR UNDER

Little Red Riding Hood buying
a bottle of wine for grandma

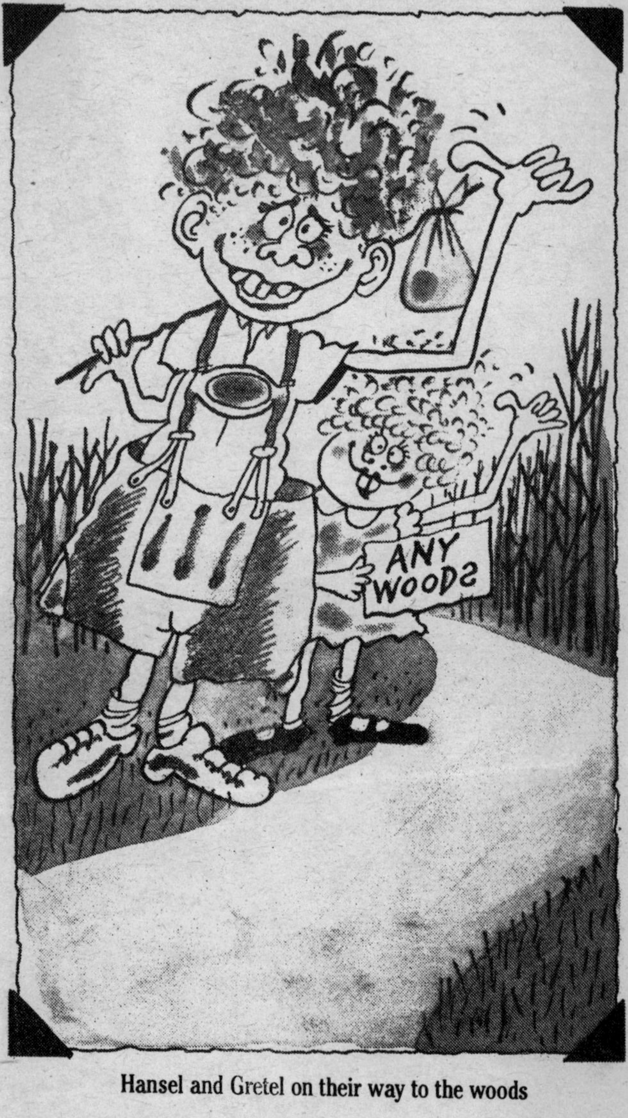
ANY
WOODS

Hansel and Gretel on their way to the woods

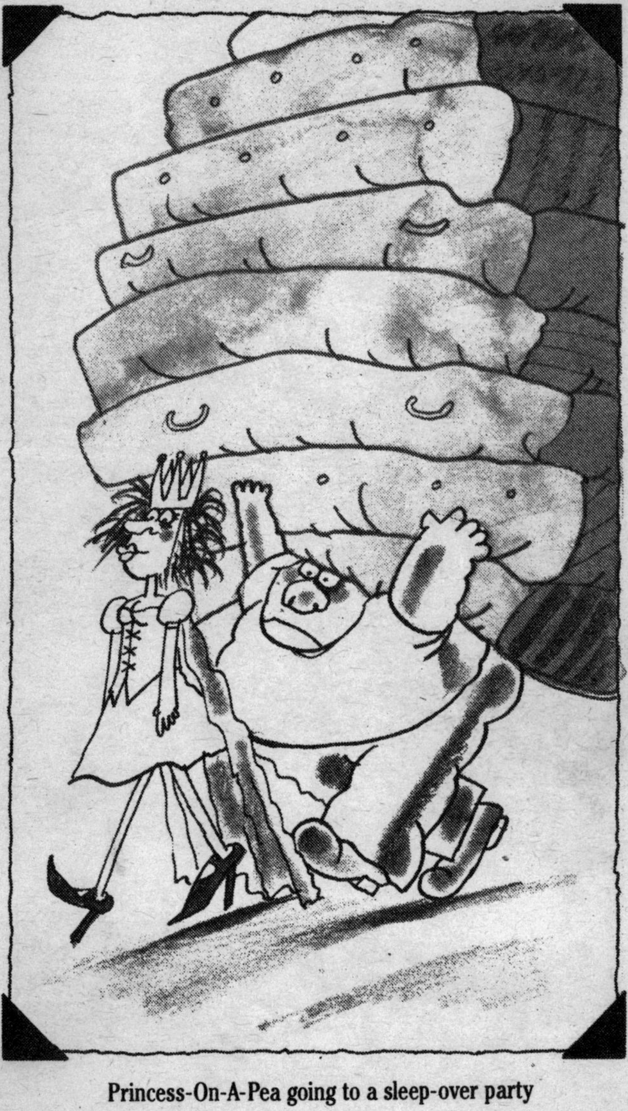

Princess-On-A-Pea going to a sleep-over party

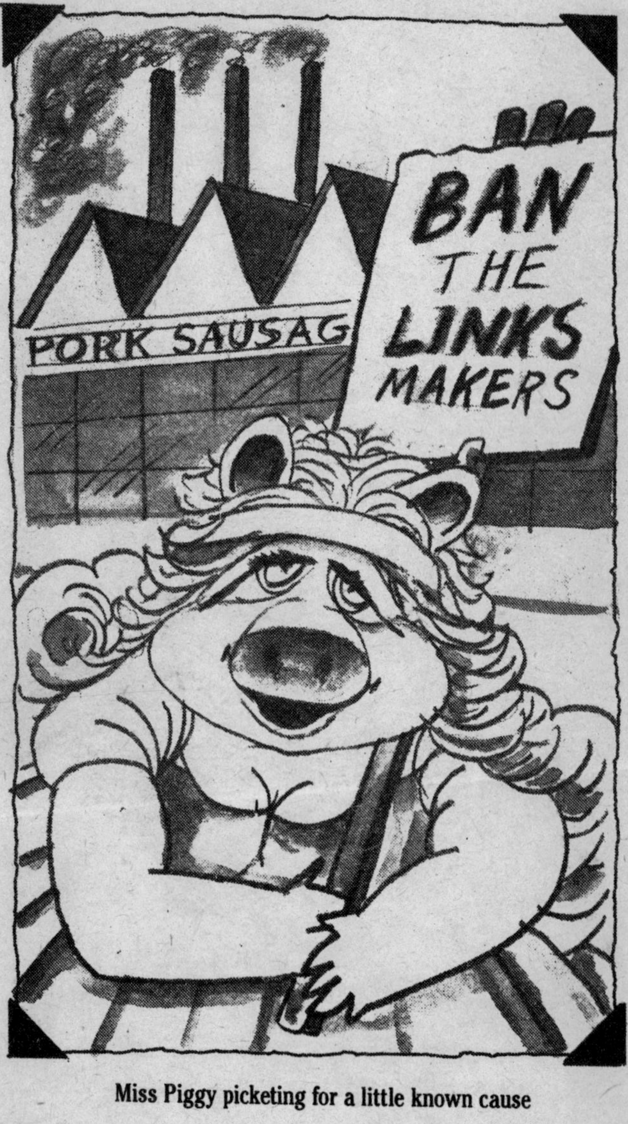
PORK SAUSAG
BAN
THE
LINKS
MAKERS

Miss Piggy picketing for a little known cause

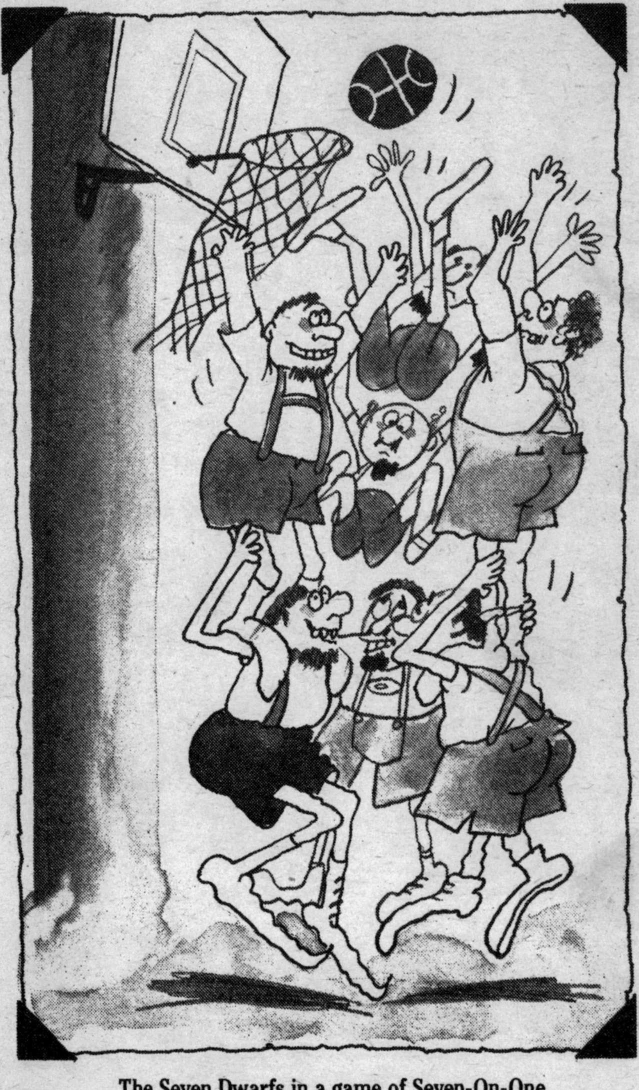

The Seven Dwarfs in a game of Seven-On-One

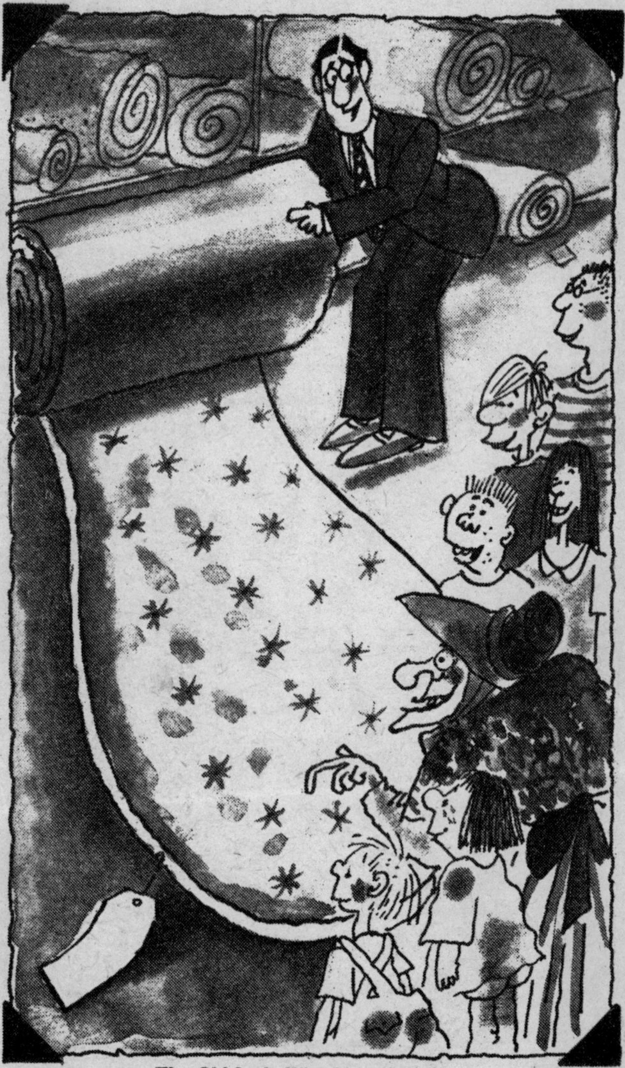

The Old Lady Who Lives In A Shoe
shopping for a new wall-to-wall Odor Eater

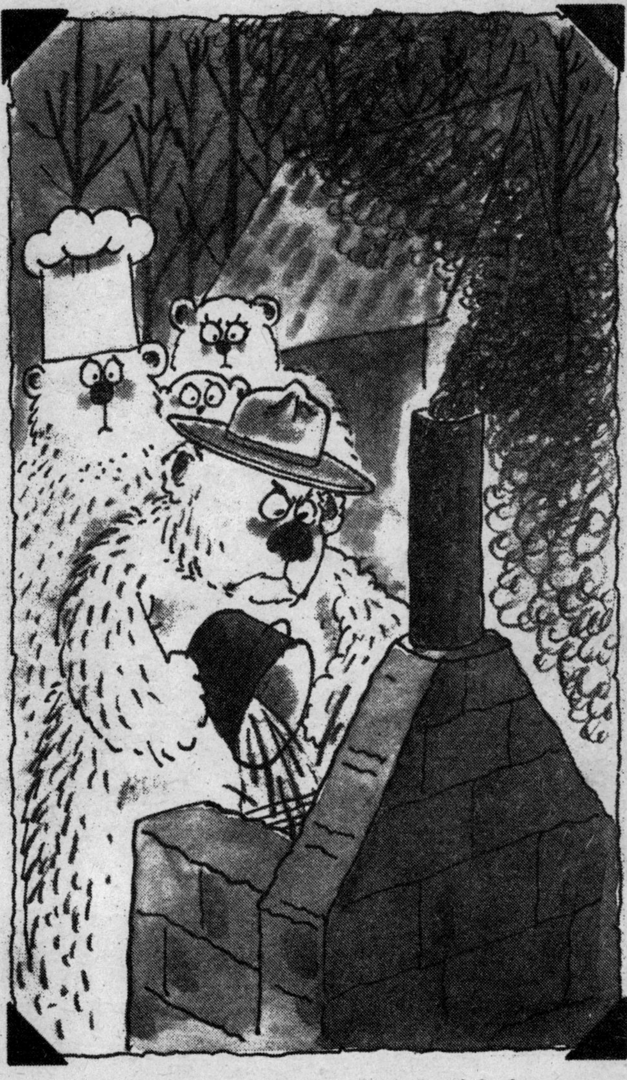

Smokey interrupting the Three Little Bear's barbecue

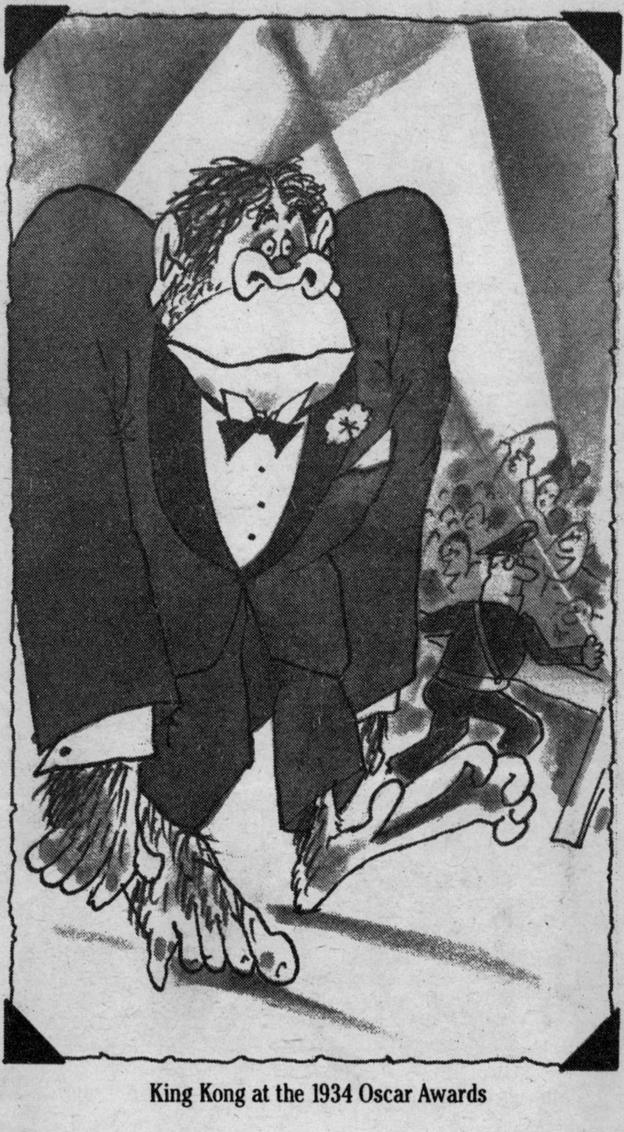

King Kong at the 1934 Oscar Awards

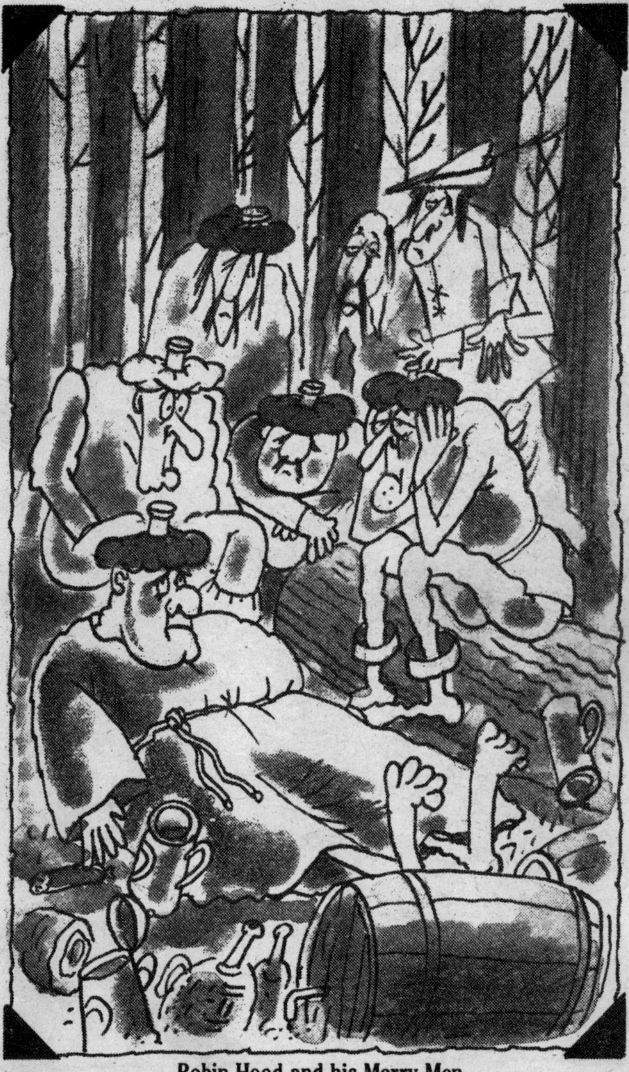

Robin Hood and his Merry Men
after a night of merrymaking

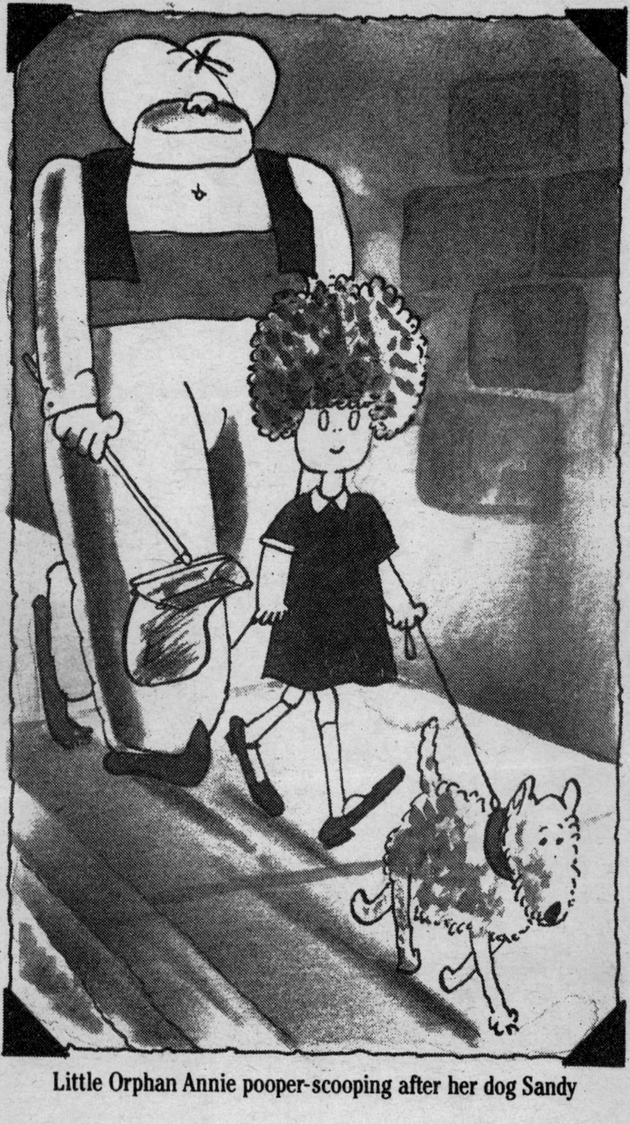

Little Orphan Annie pooper-scooping after her dog Sandy

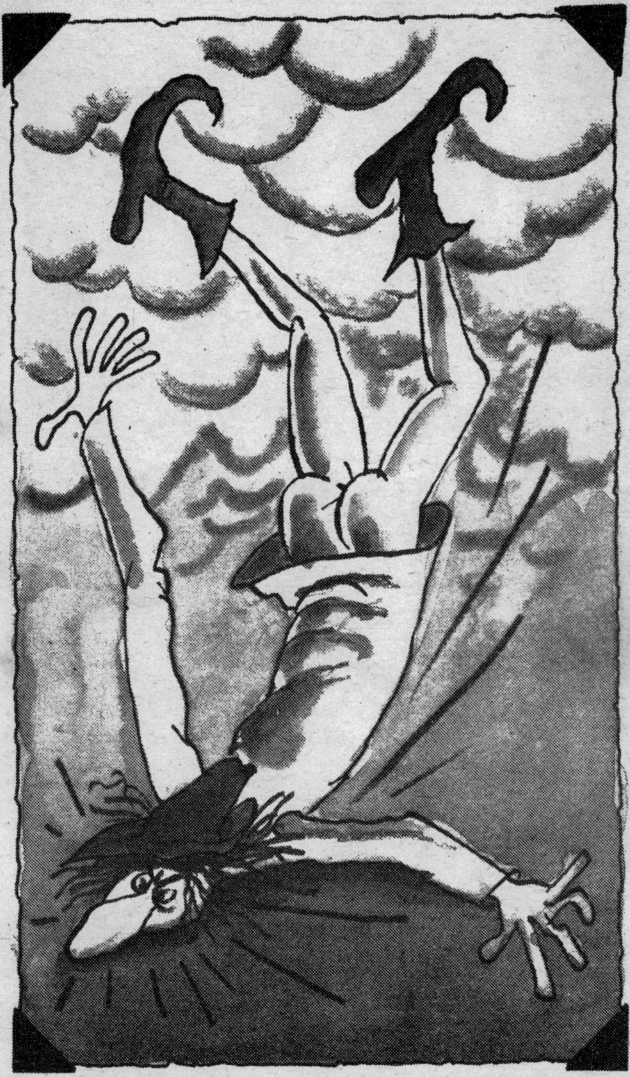

Peter Pan making a one point landing in bad weather

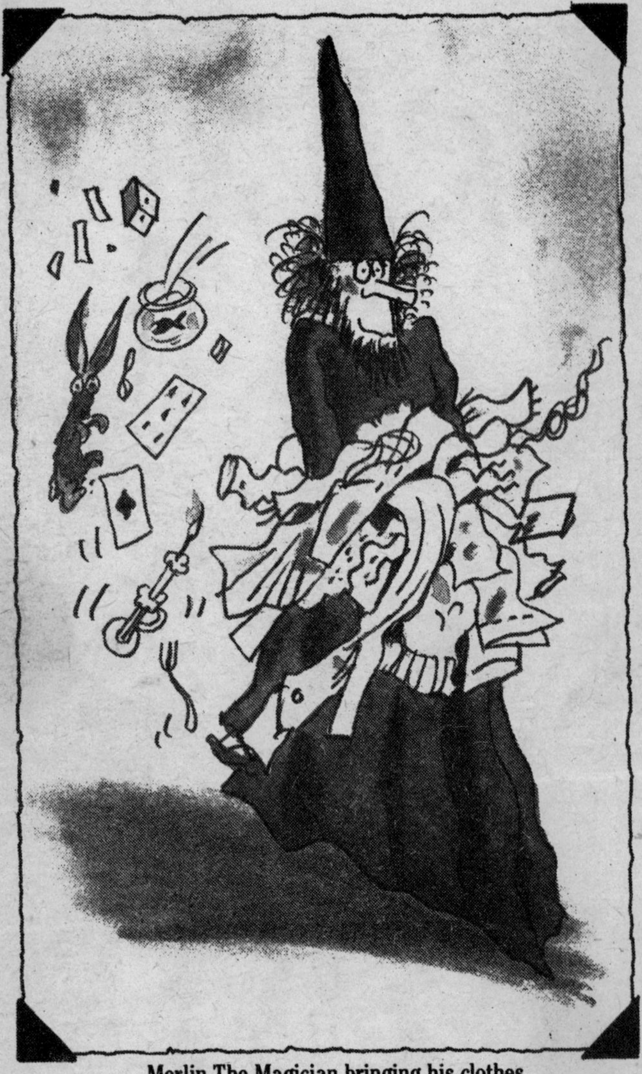

Merlin The Magician bringing his clothes
to the dry-cleaners

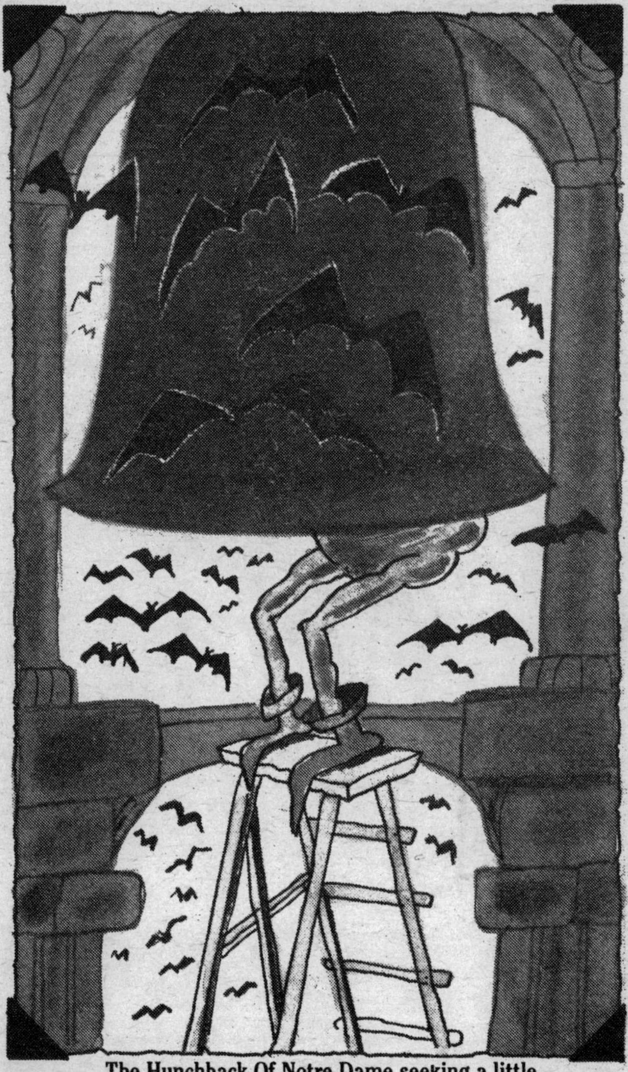

The Hunchback Of Notre Dame seeking a little privacy from his fellow tower dwellers

MAD
PHOTO
FINISHES

THE SCENE:

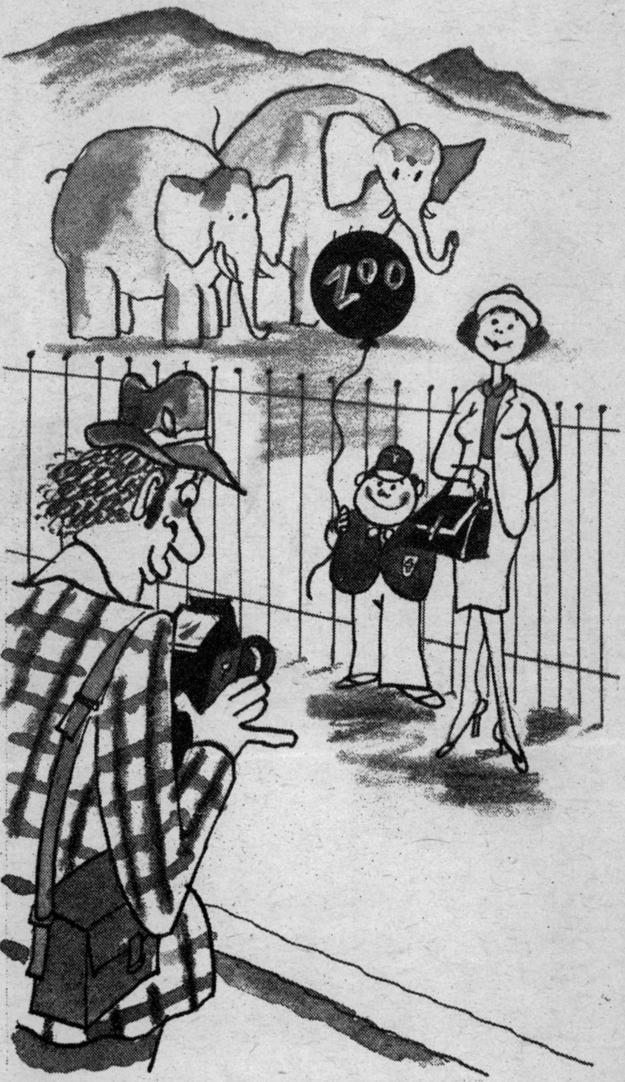
ZOO

THE FINISHED PHOTO:

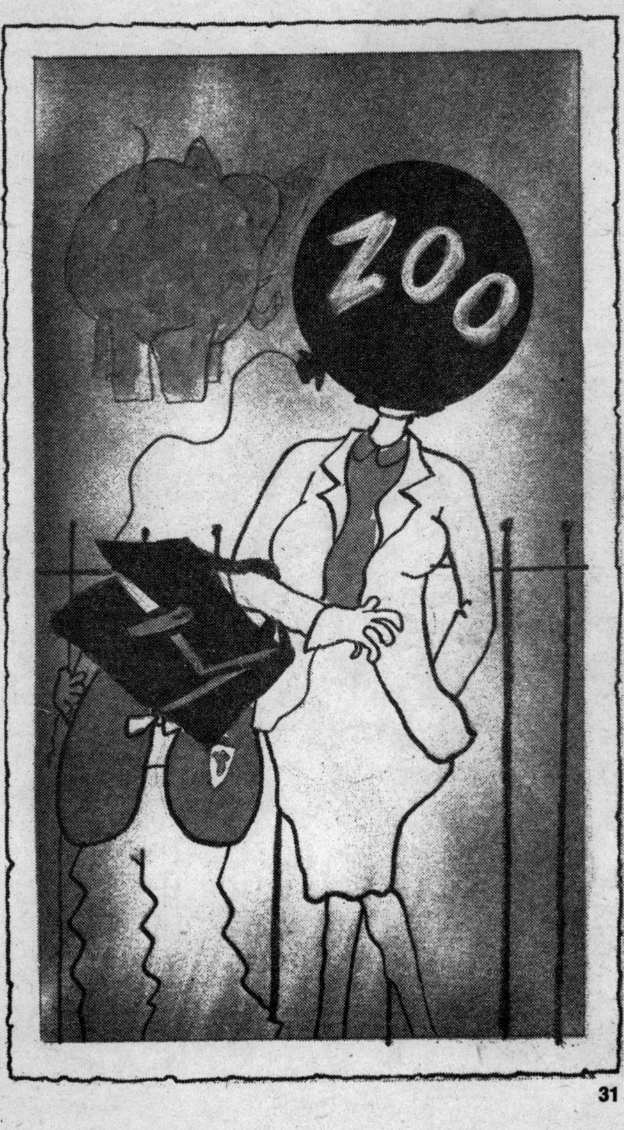
ZOO

THE SCENE:

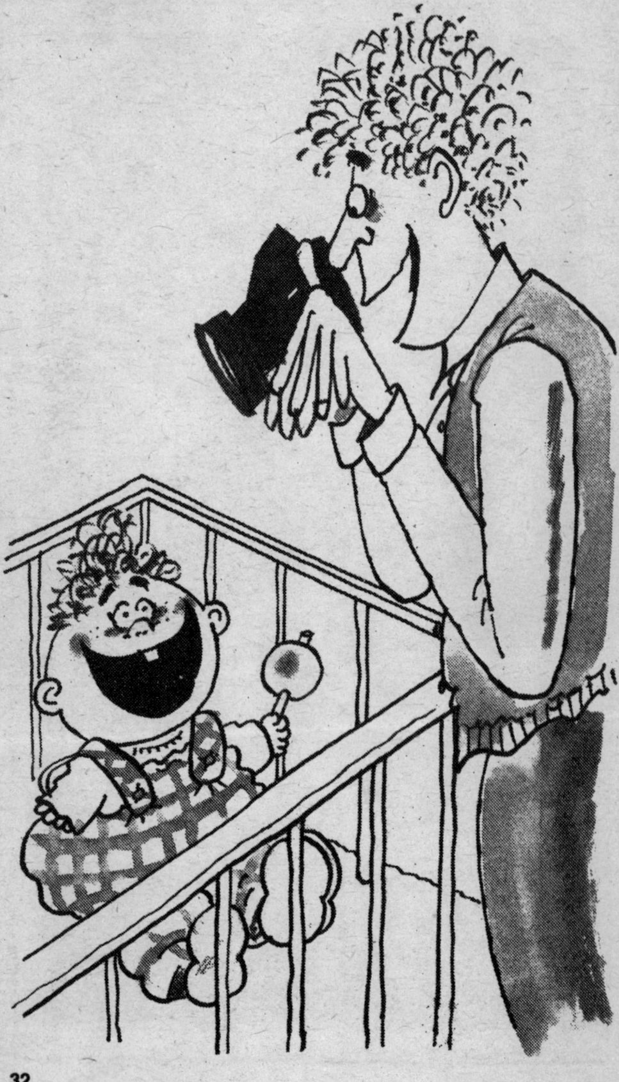

THE FINISHED PHOTO:

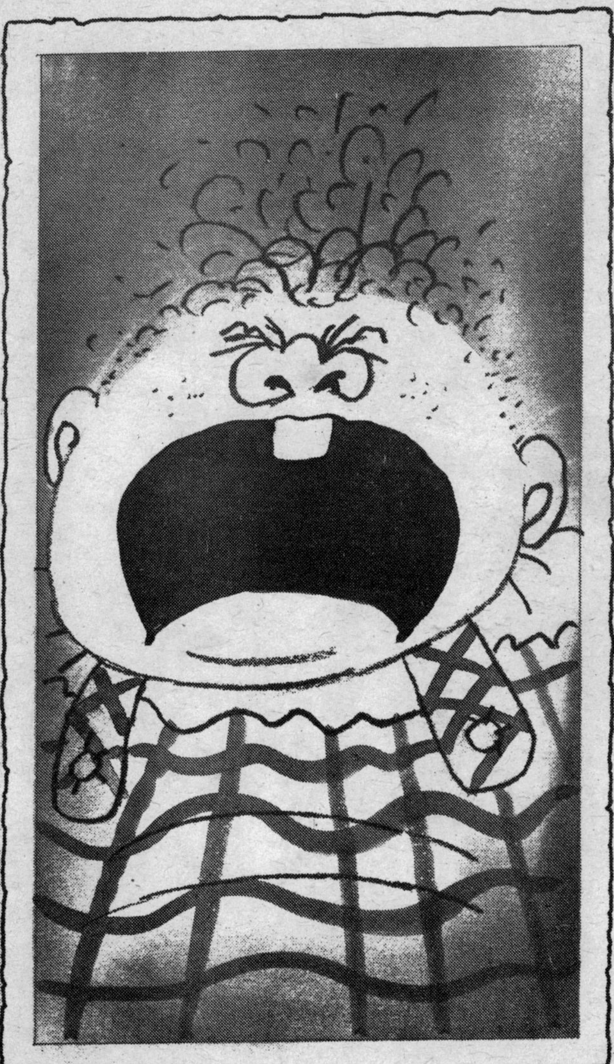

THE SCENE:

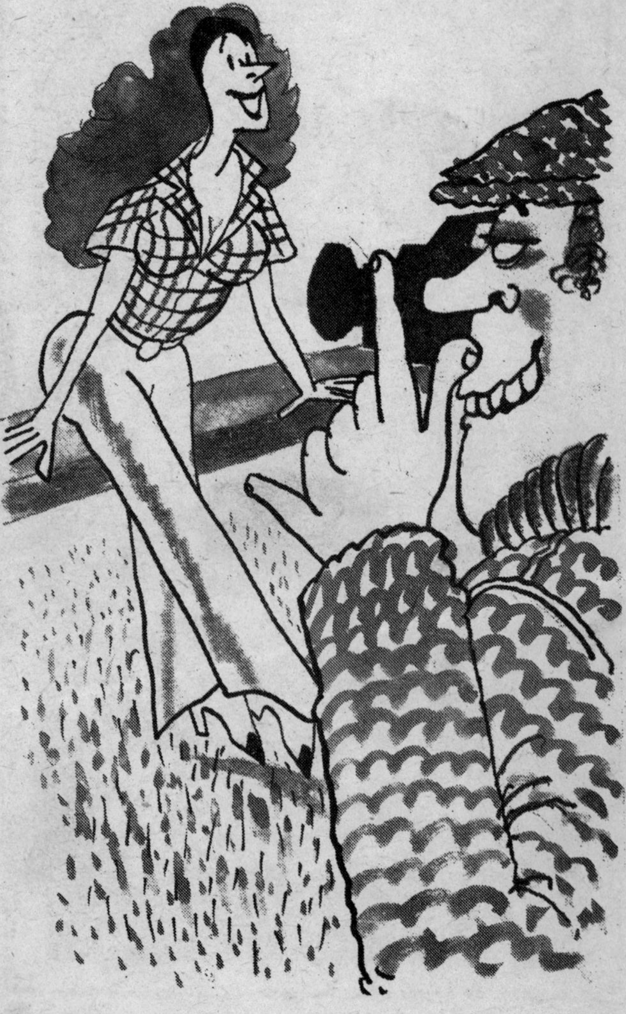

THE FINISHED PHOTO:

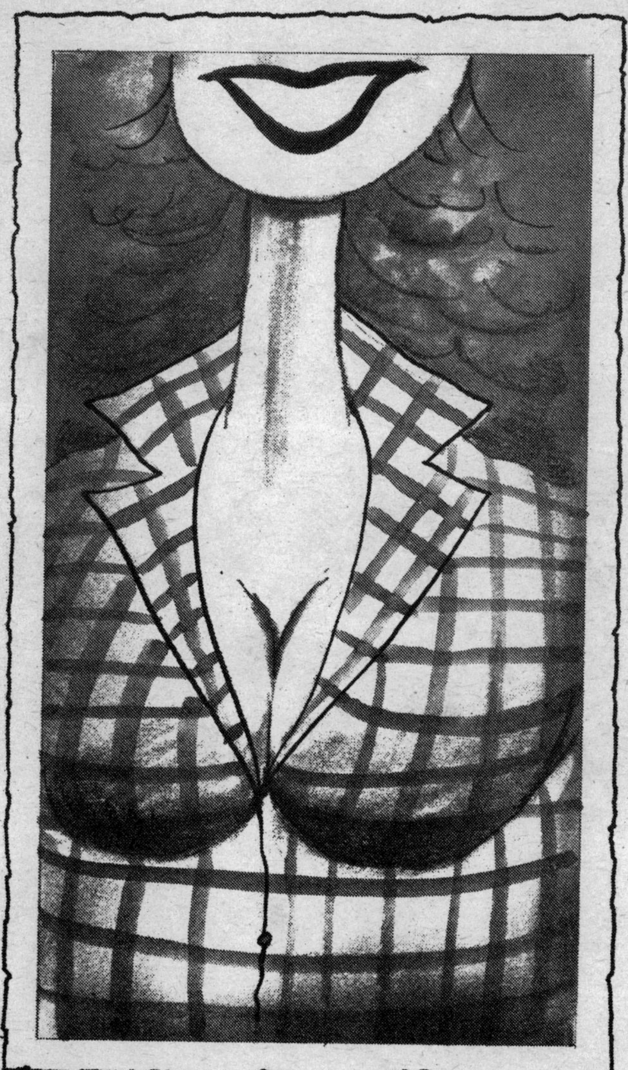

THE SCENE:

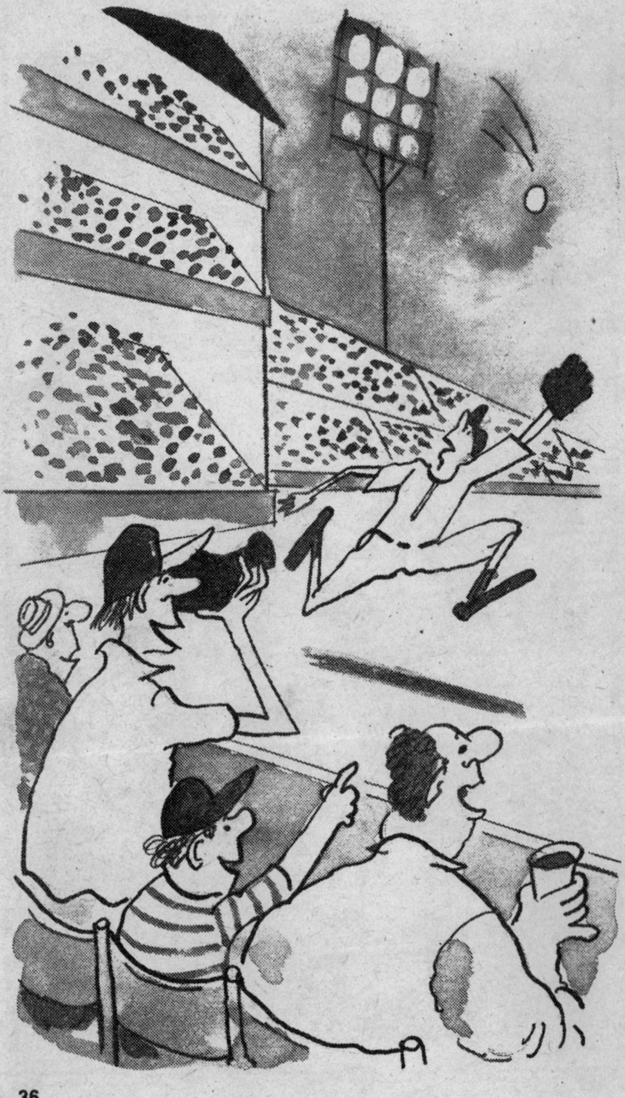

THE FINISHED PHOTO:

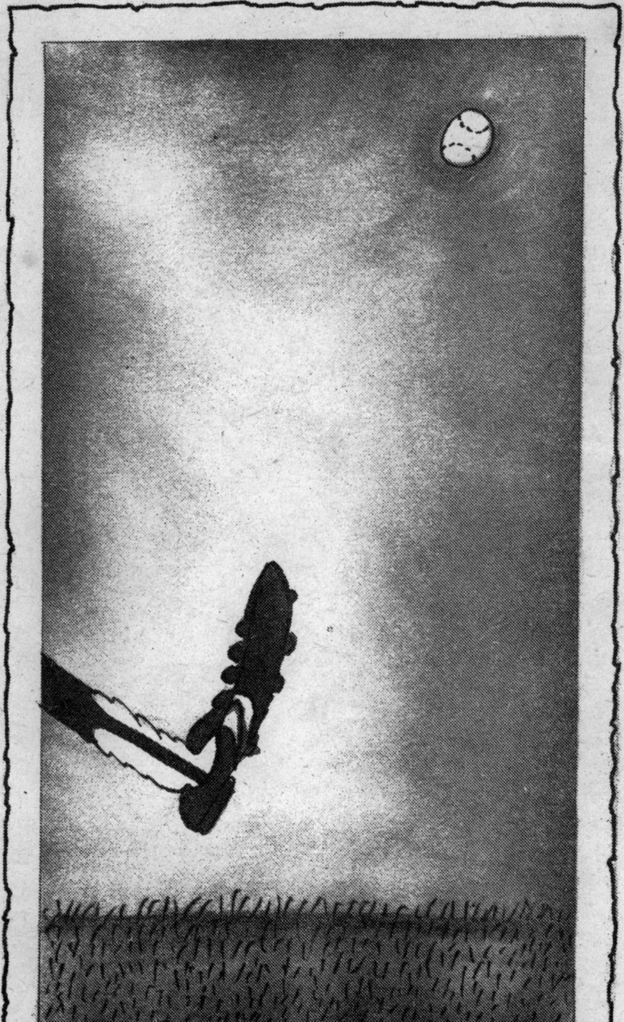

THE SCENE:

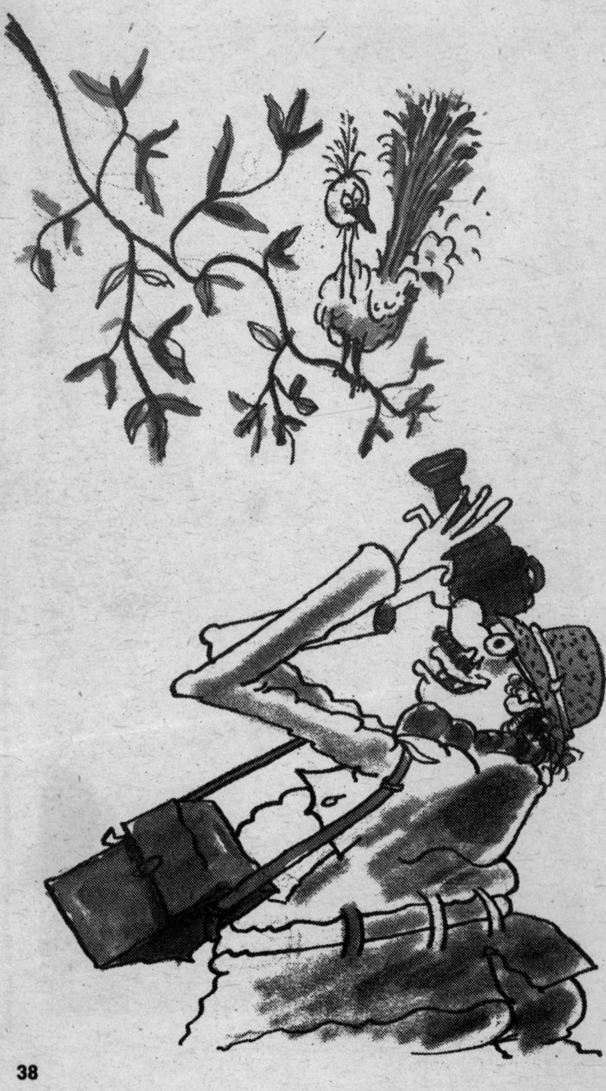

THE FINISHED PHOTO:

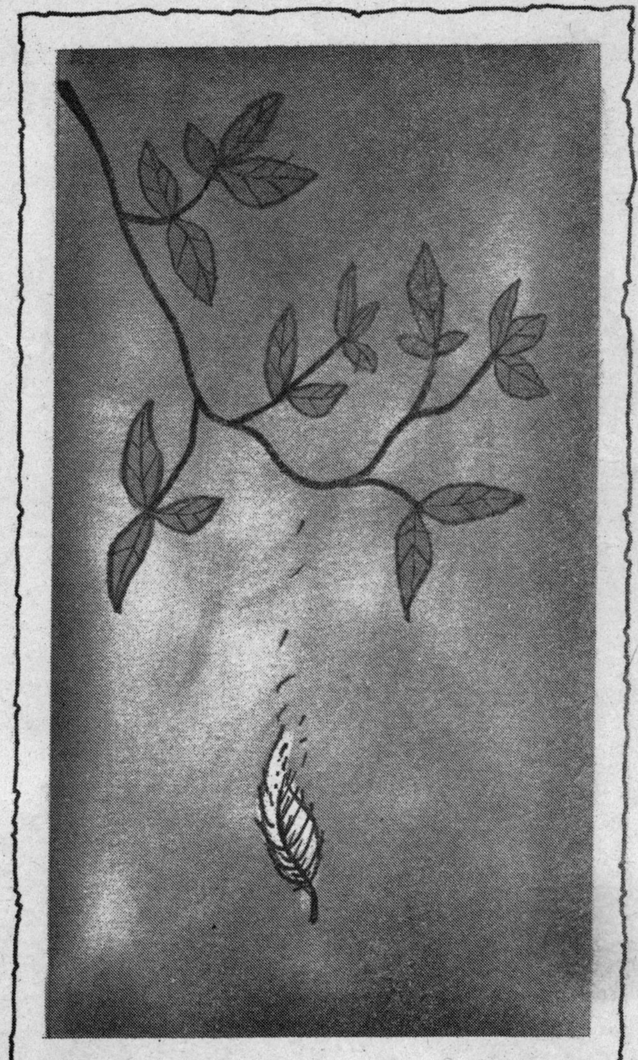

THE SCENE:

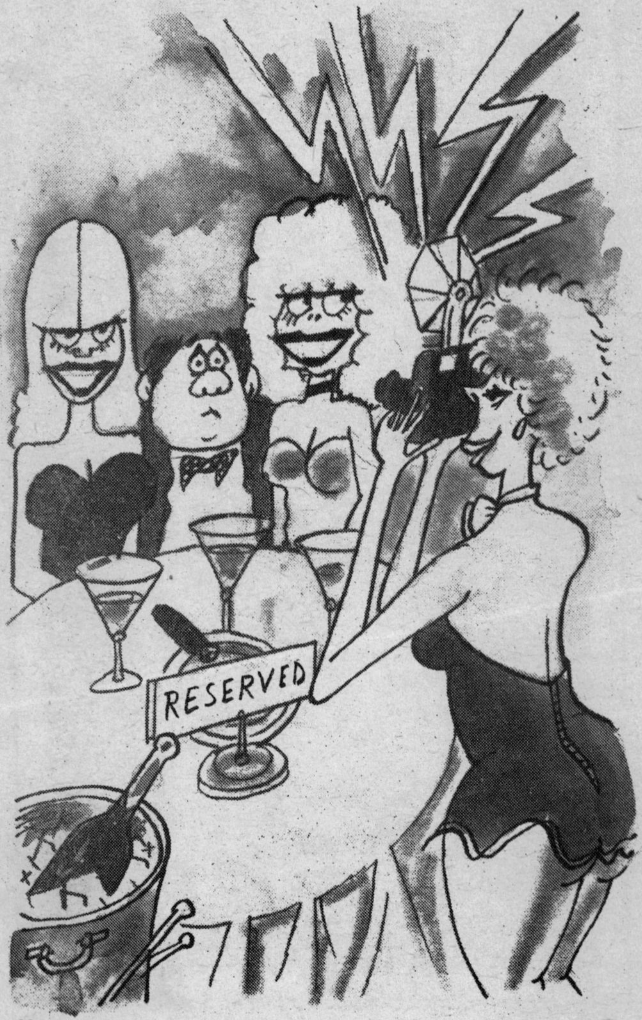
RESERVED

THE FINISHED PHOTO:

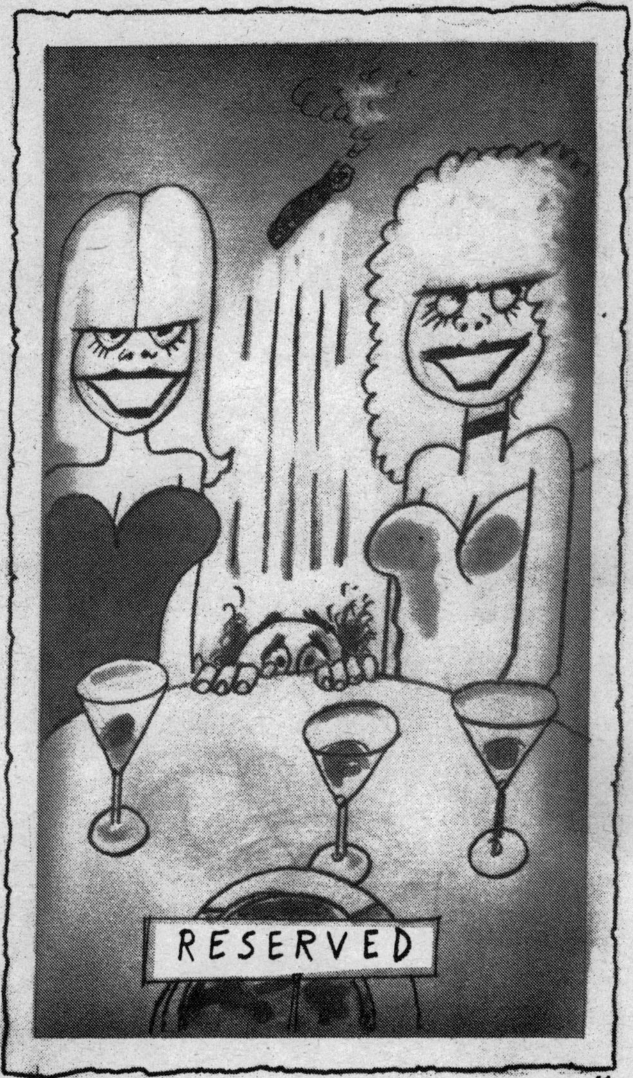
RESERVED

THE SCENE:

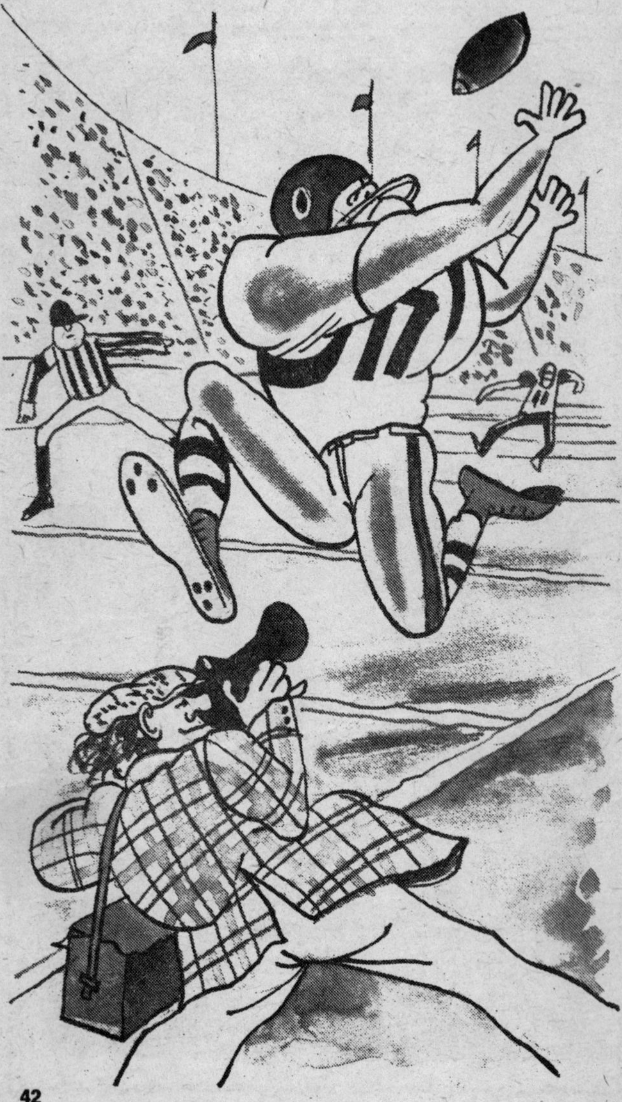

THE FINISHED PHOTO:

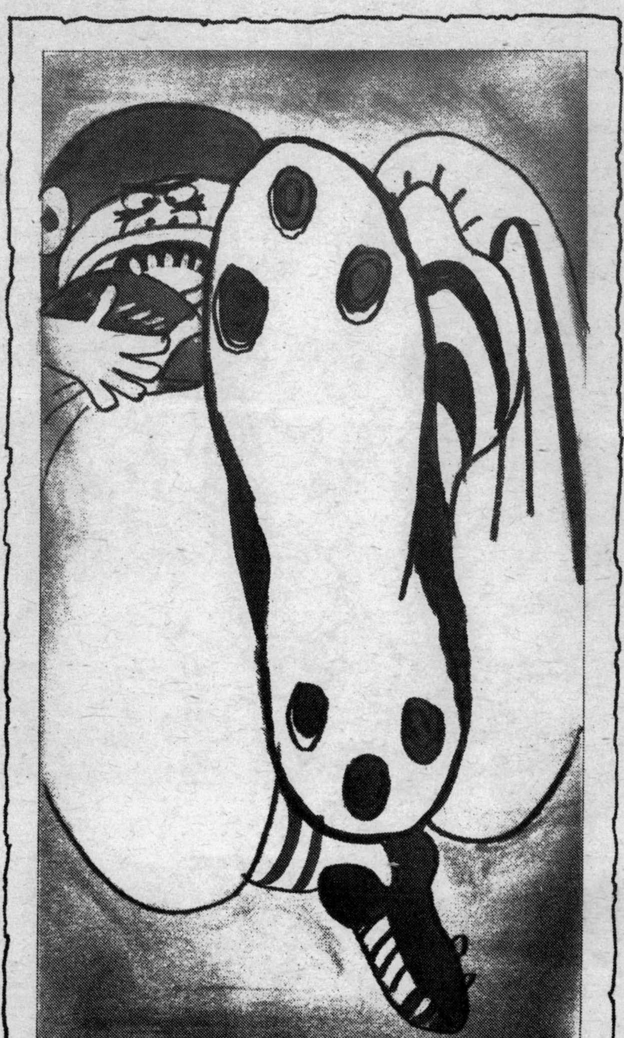

THE SCENE:

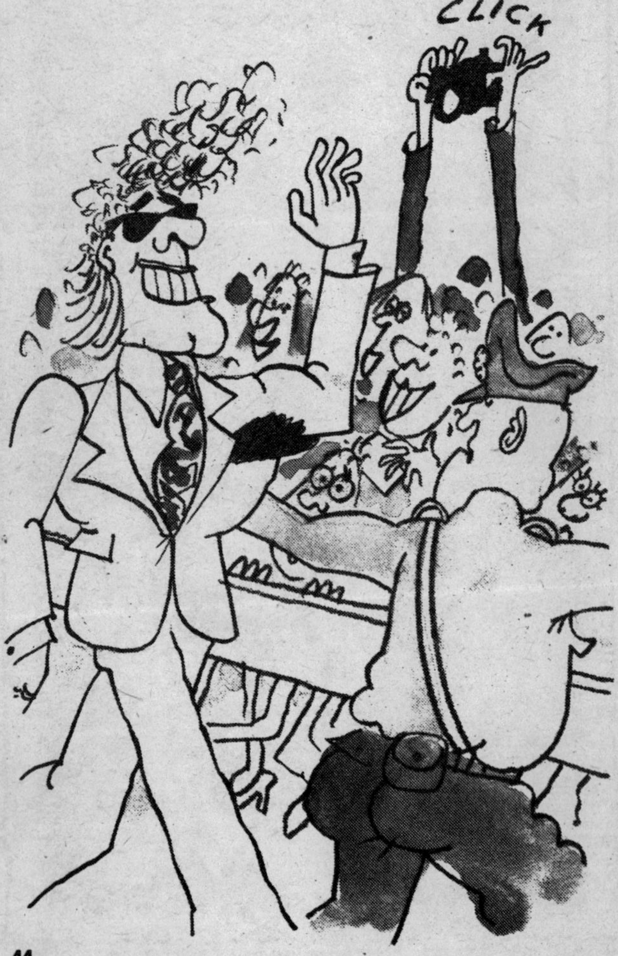
CLICK

THE FINISHED PHOTO:

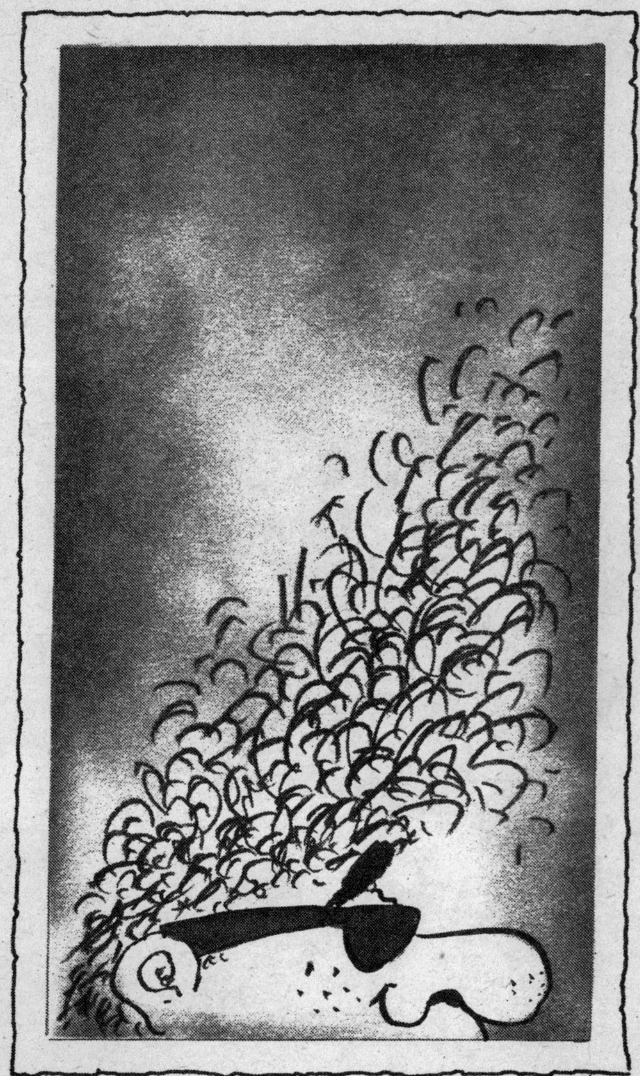

AN ALBUM OF UNFORGET-TABLE (*YAWN*) VACATION PICTURES

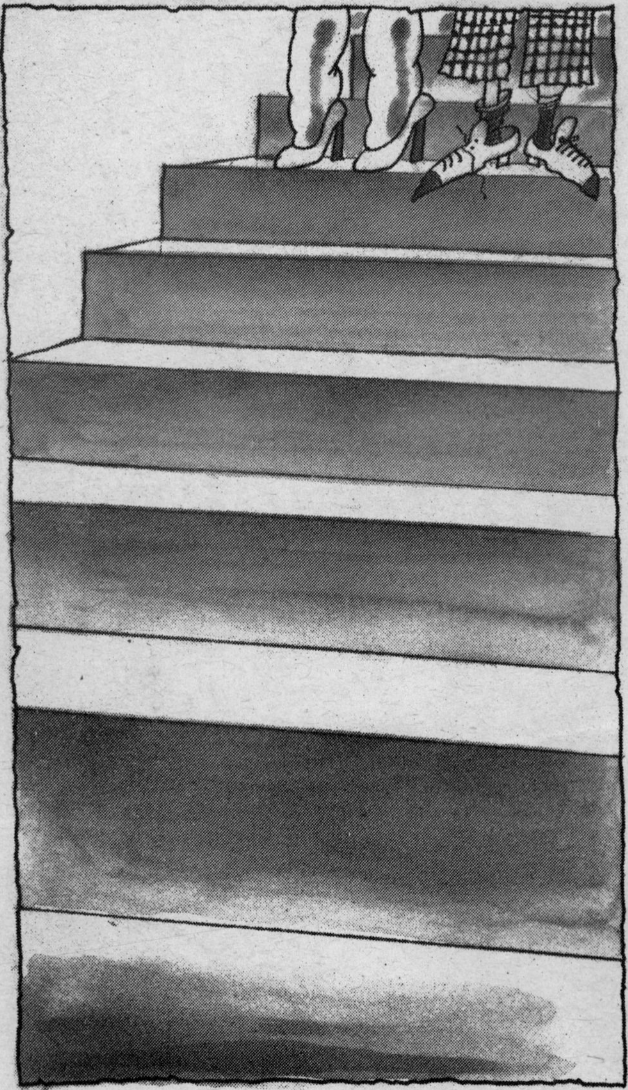

THE SPANISH STEPS IN ROME

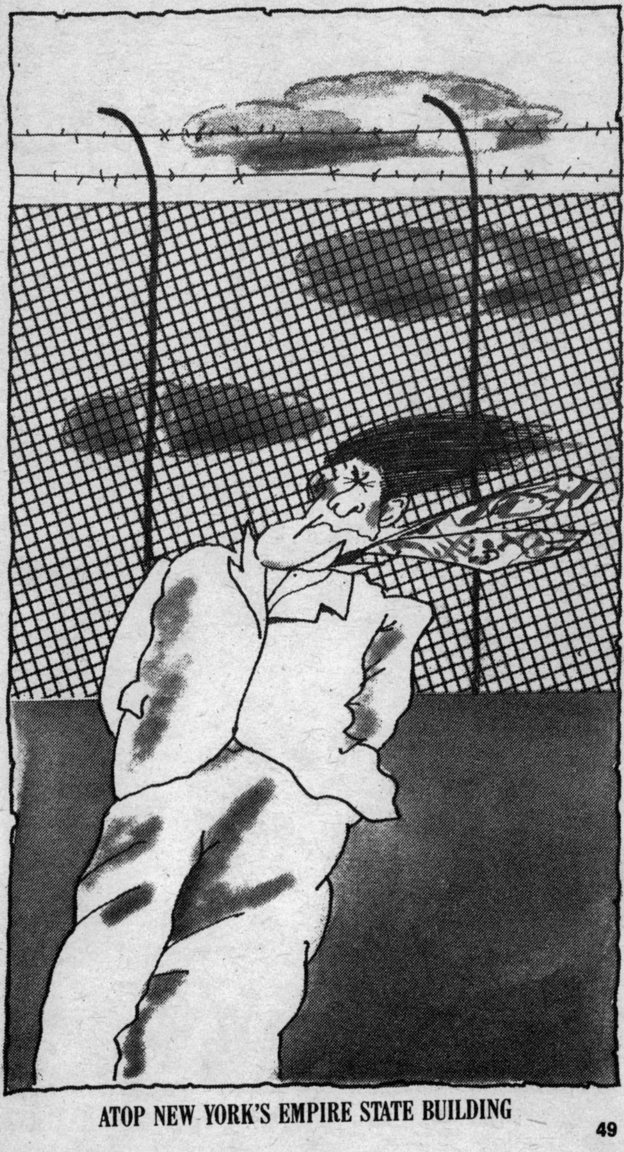

ATOP NEW YORK'S EMPIRE STATE BUILDING

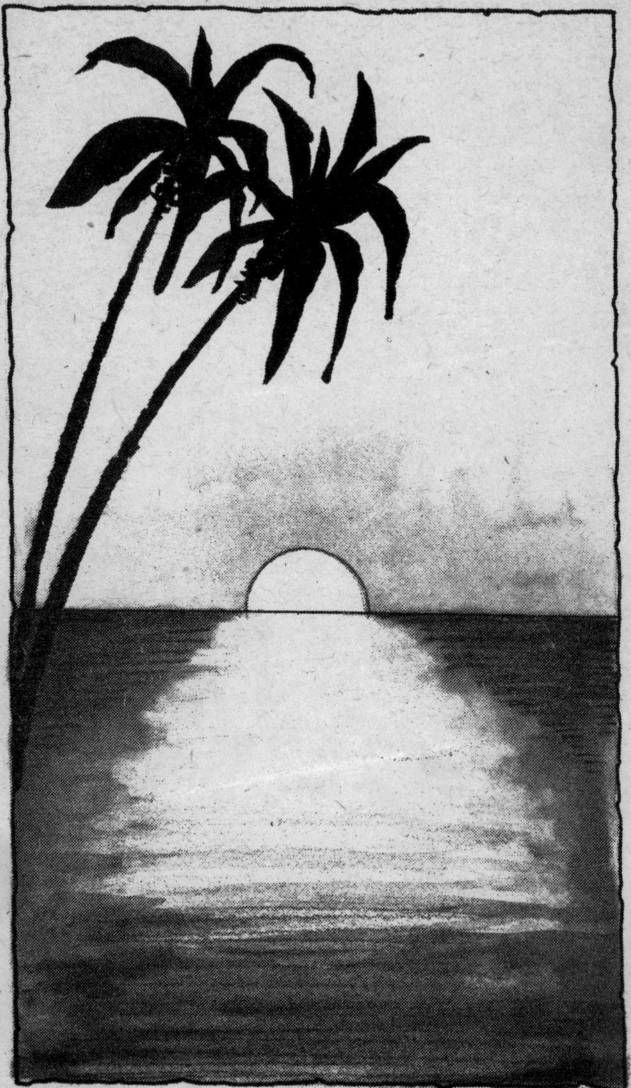

SUNSET IN THE SOUTH PACIFIC? CARIBBEAN? MEDITERRANEAN?

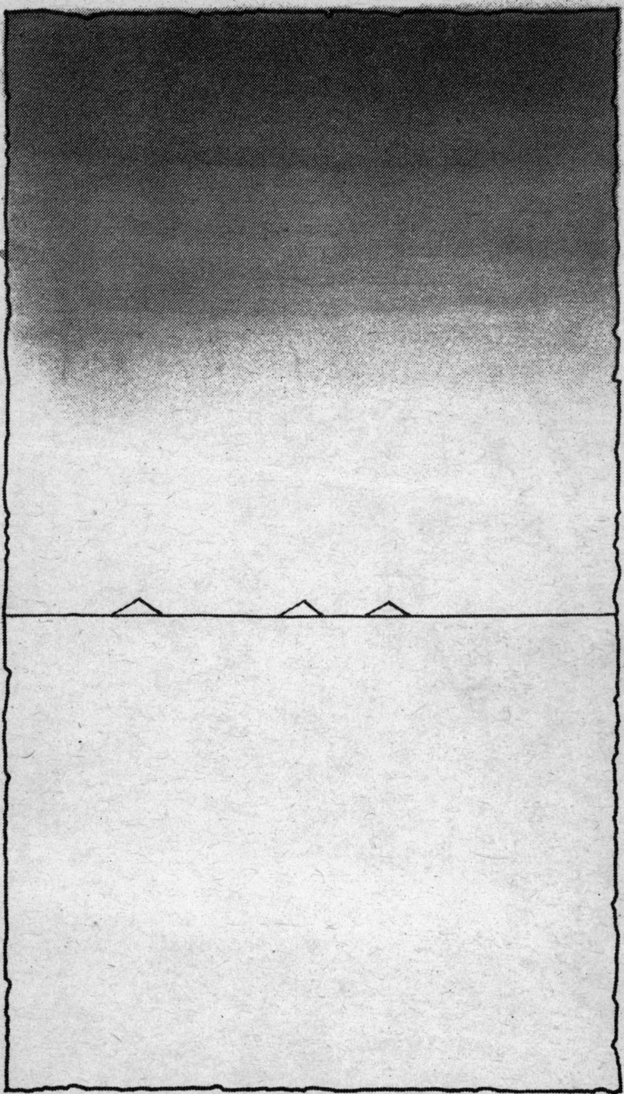

A WIDE-ANGLE SHOT OF THE PYRAMIDS

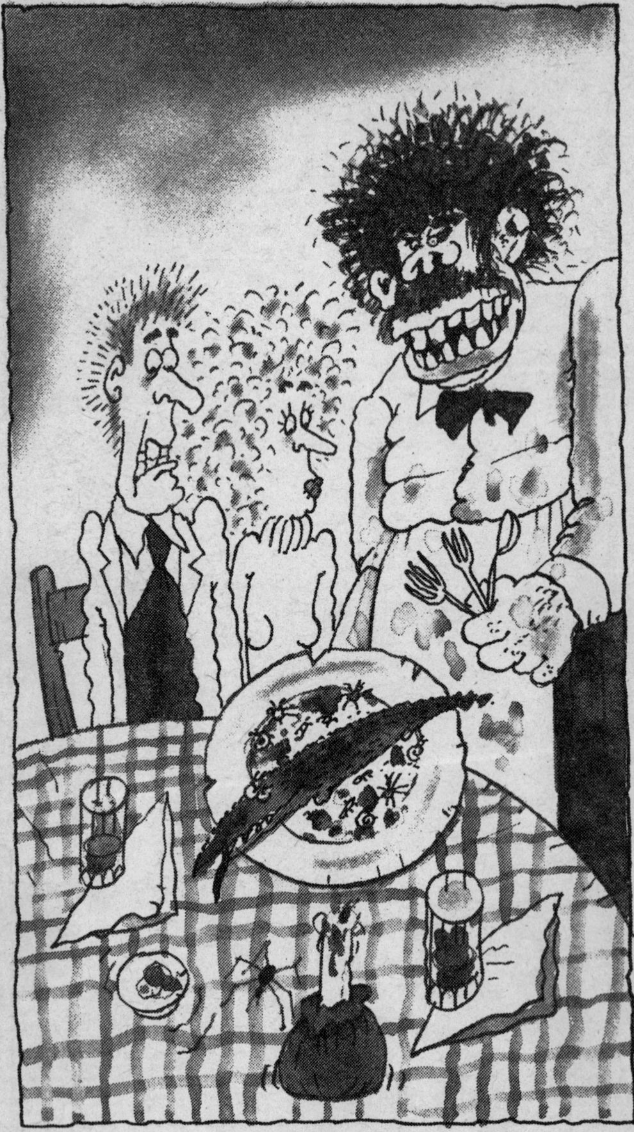

EATING A NATIVE MEAL

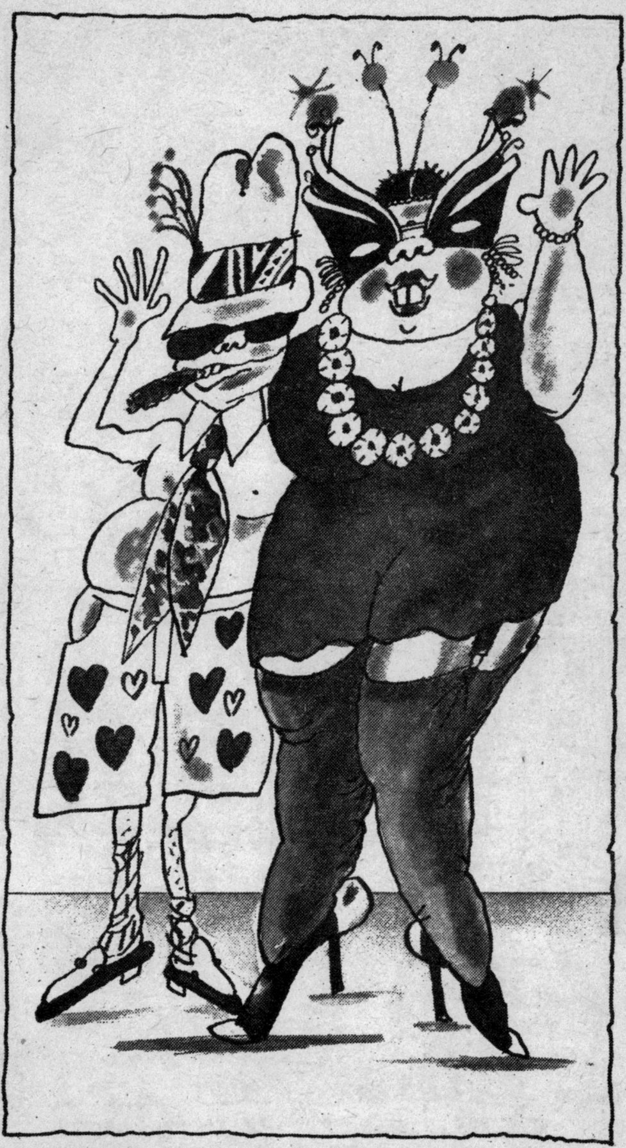

RUNNERS-UP AT THE S.S. MALDEMER COSTUME PARTY

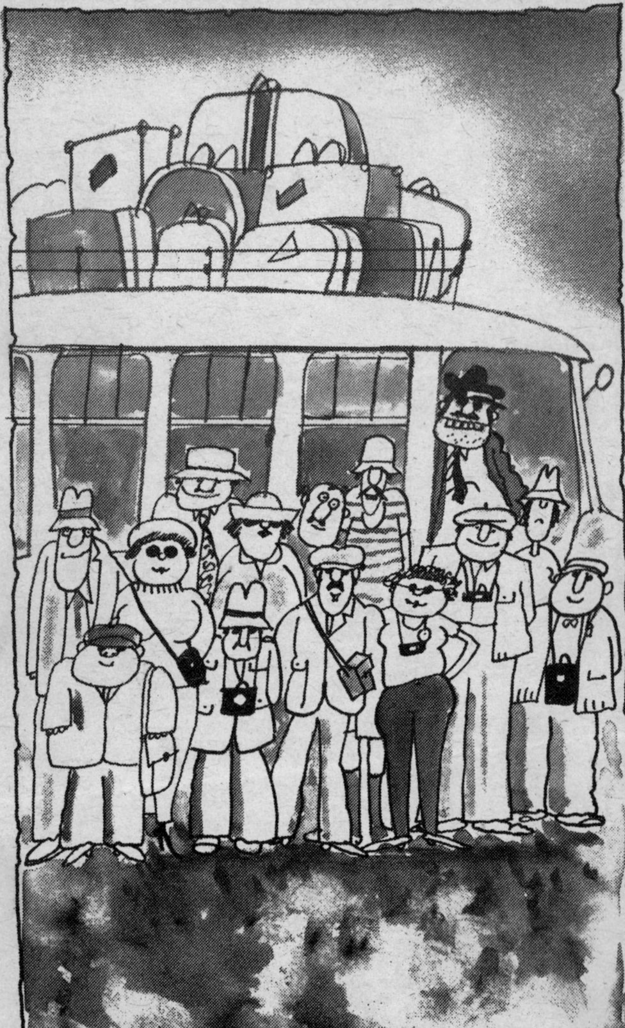

MEMBERS OF OUR TOUR WITH CARLOS THE DRIVER

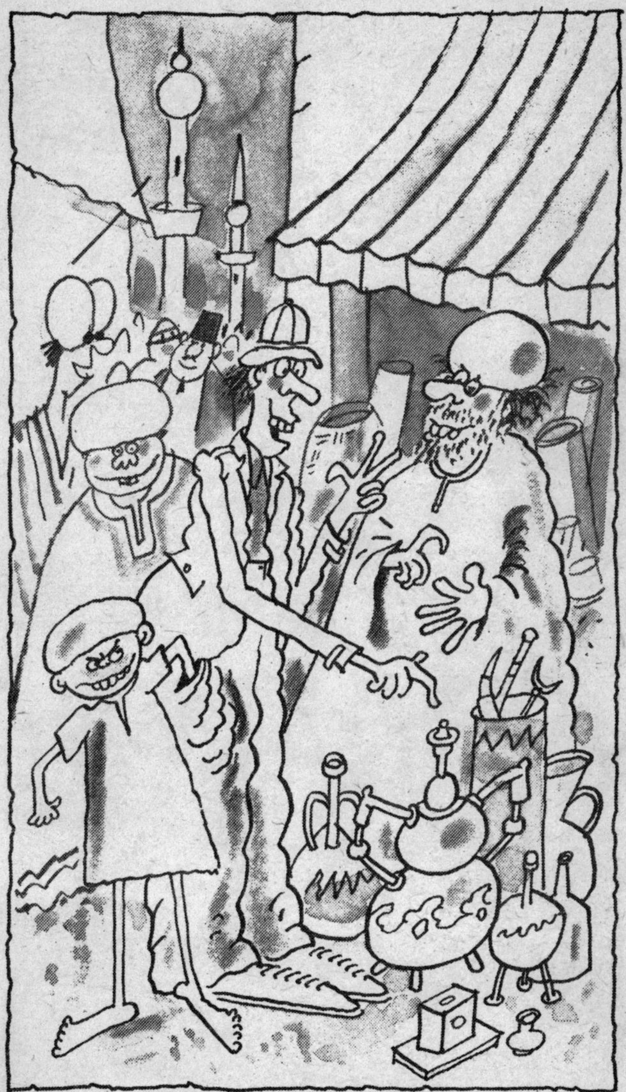

BARGAINING IN THE LOCAL BAZAAR

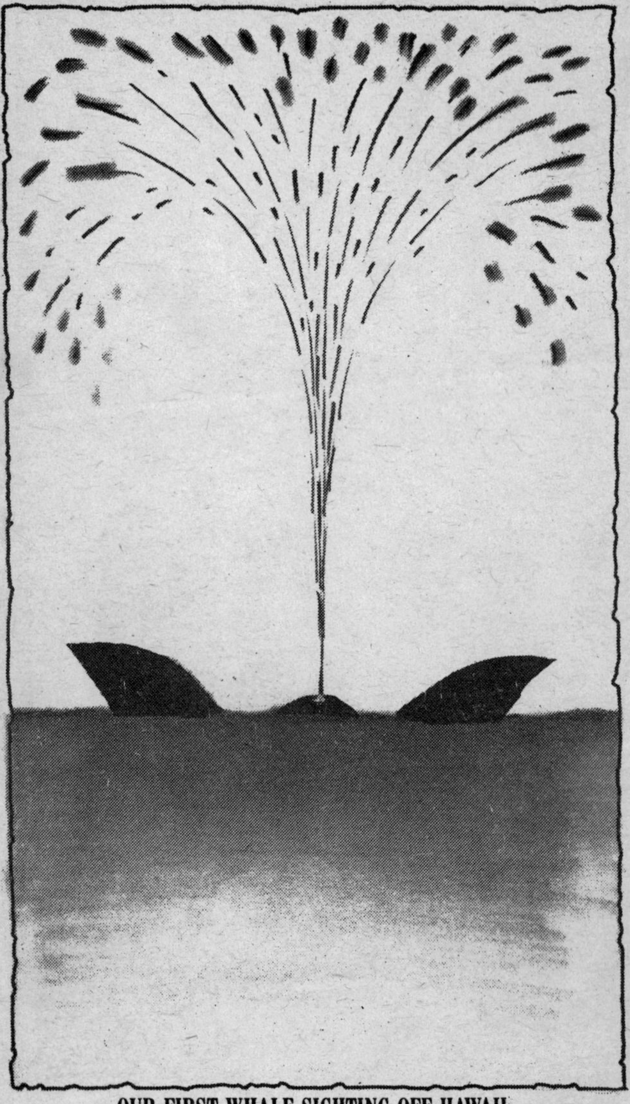

OUR FIRST WHALE SIGHTING OFF HAWAII

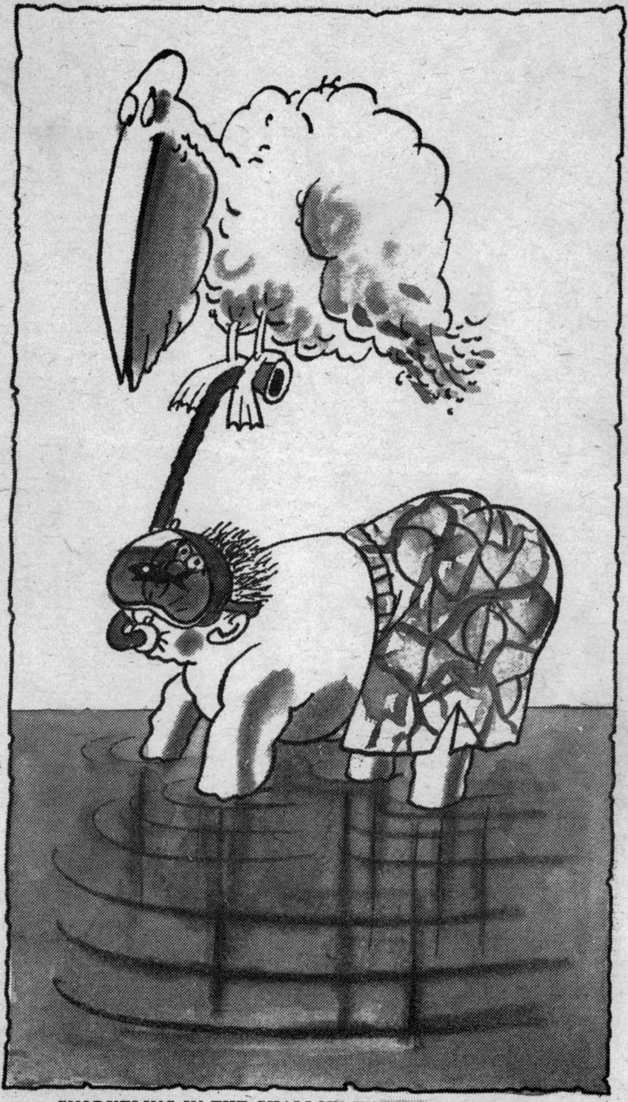

SNORKELING IN THE SHALLOW WATERS OF BERMUDA

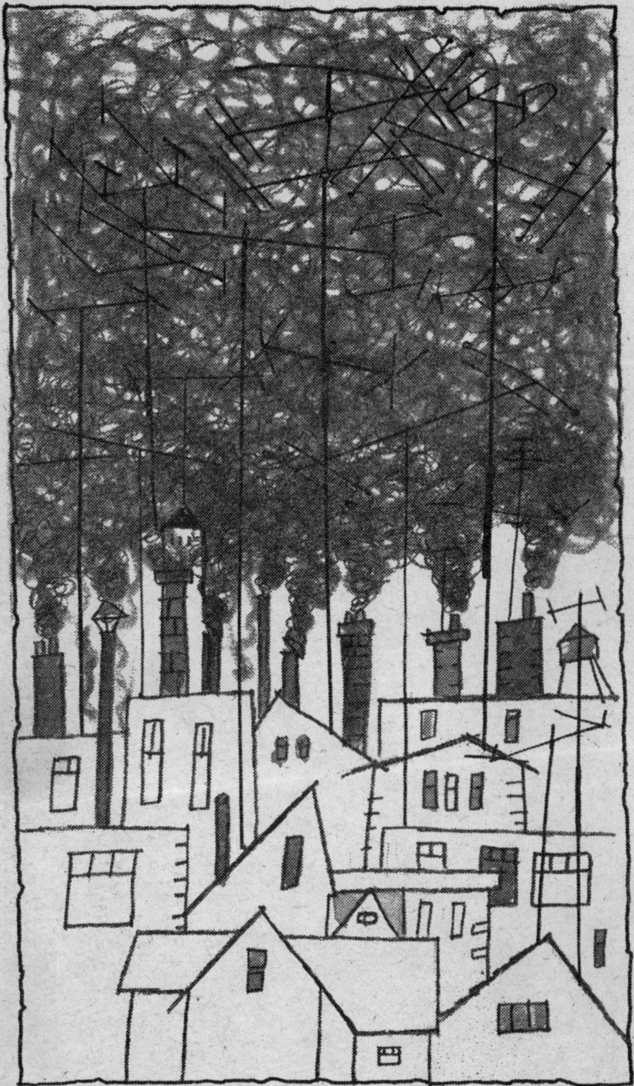

THE ROOFTOPS OF PARIS

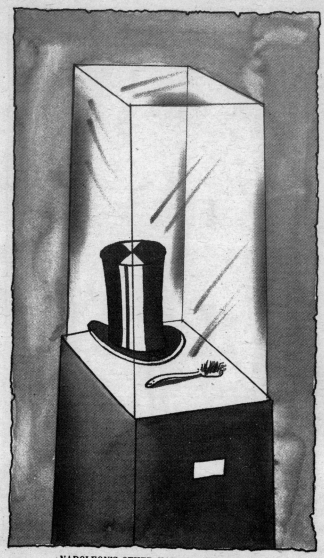

NAPOLEON'S OTHER HAT AND TOOTHBRUSH

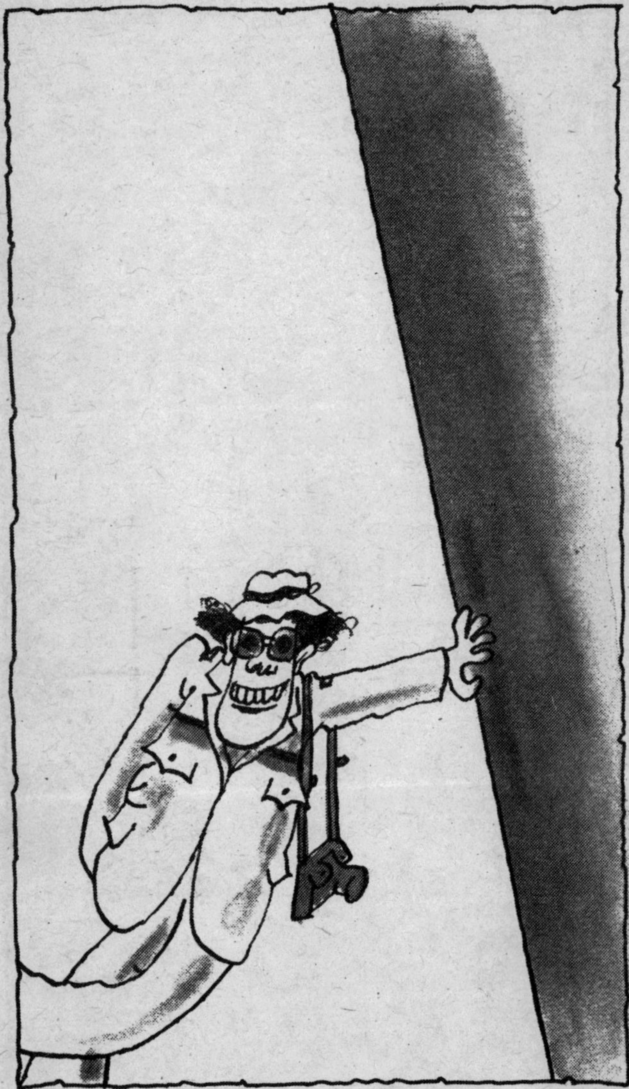

LEANING AGAINST THE TOWER OF PISA

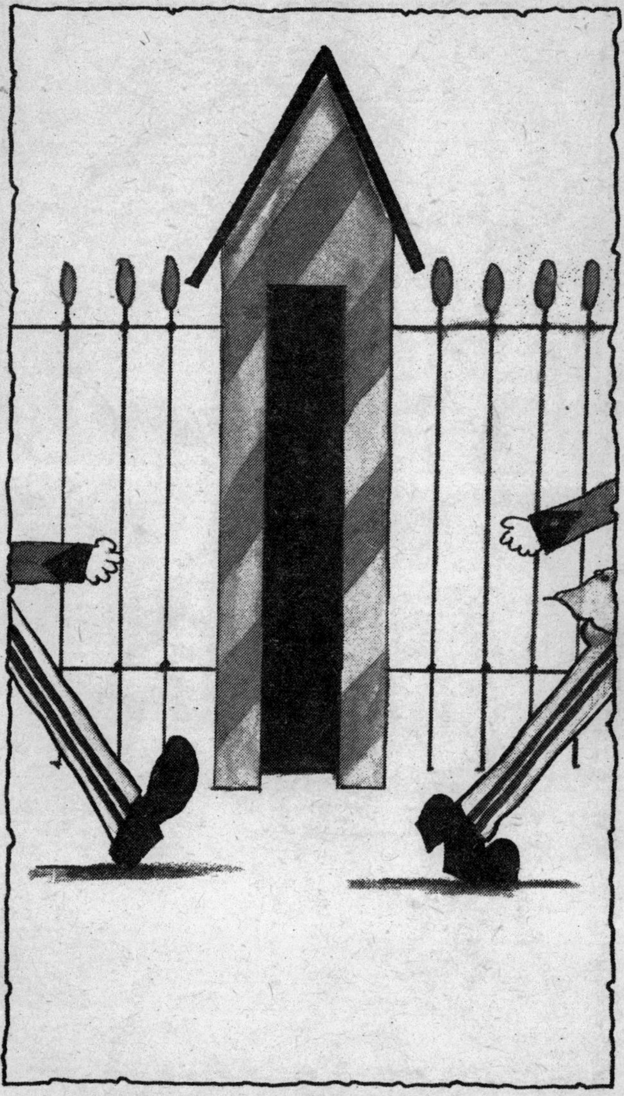

THE CHANGING OF THE GUARD AT BUCKINGHAM PALACE

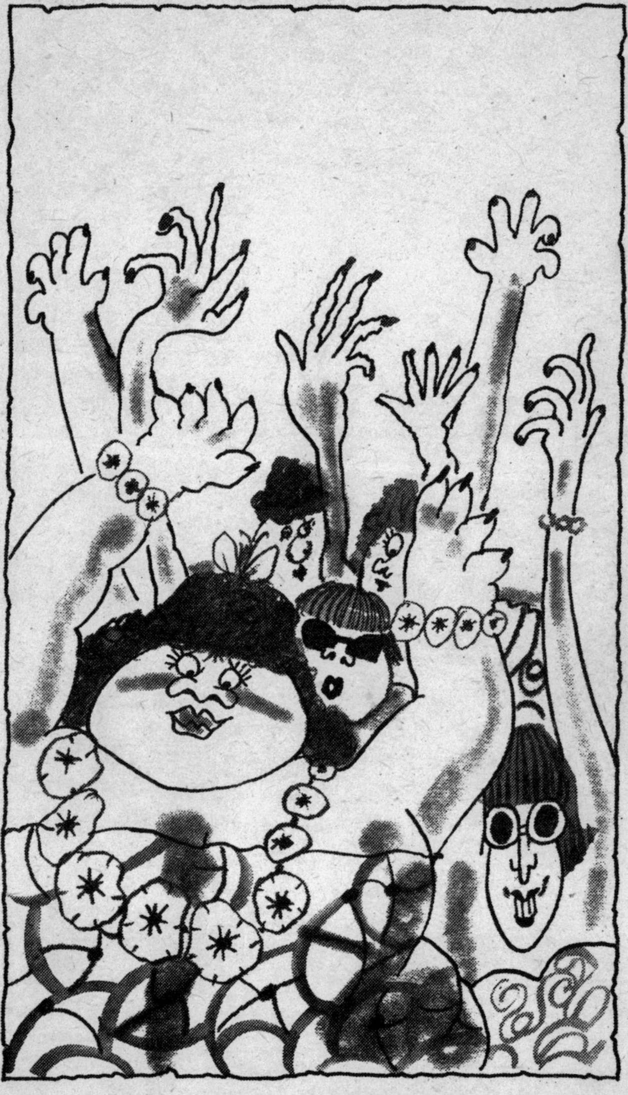

LOVELY HULA HANDS

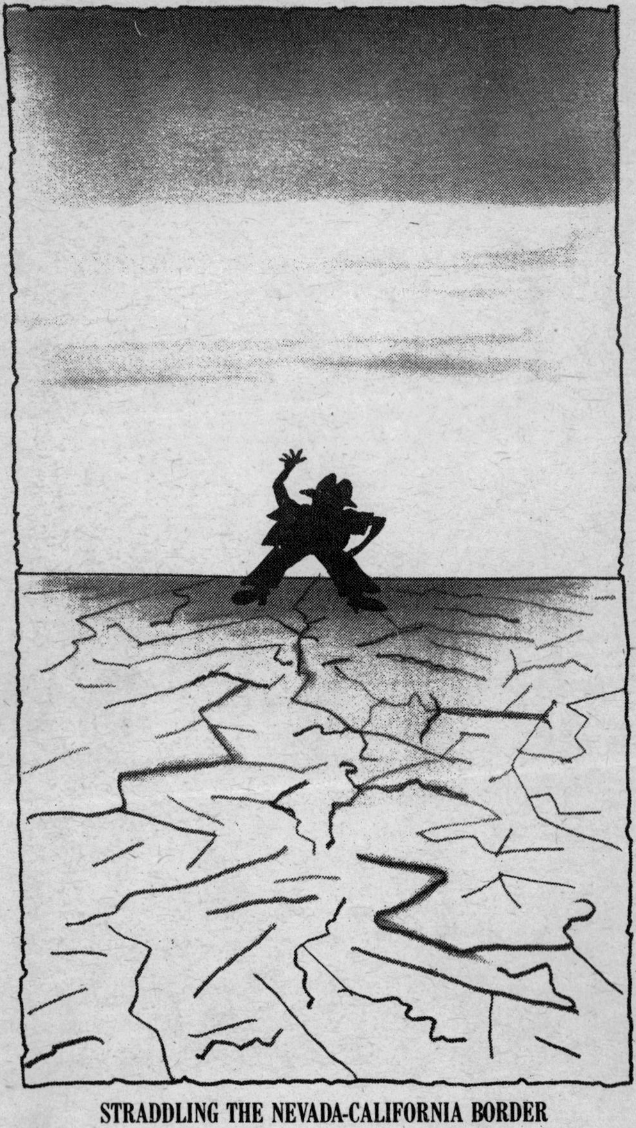

STRADDLING THE NEVADA-CALIFORNIA BORDER

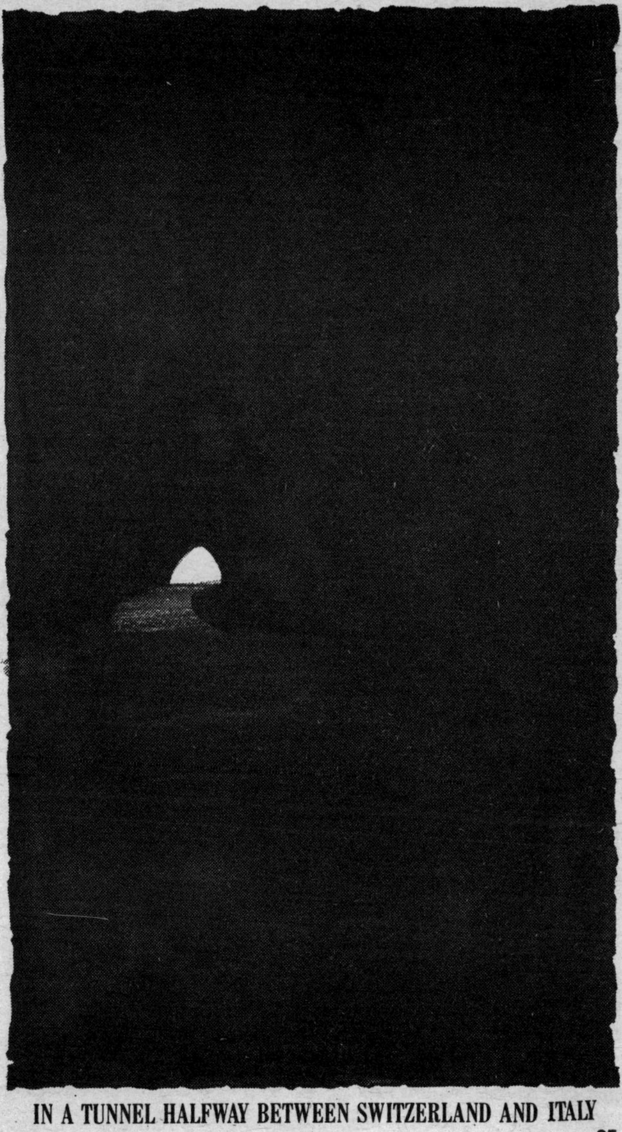

IN A TUNNEL HALFWAY BETWEEN SWITZERLAND AND ITALY

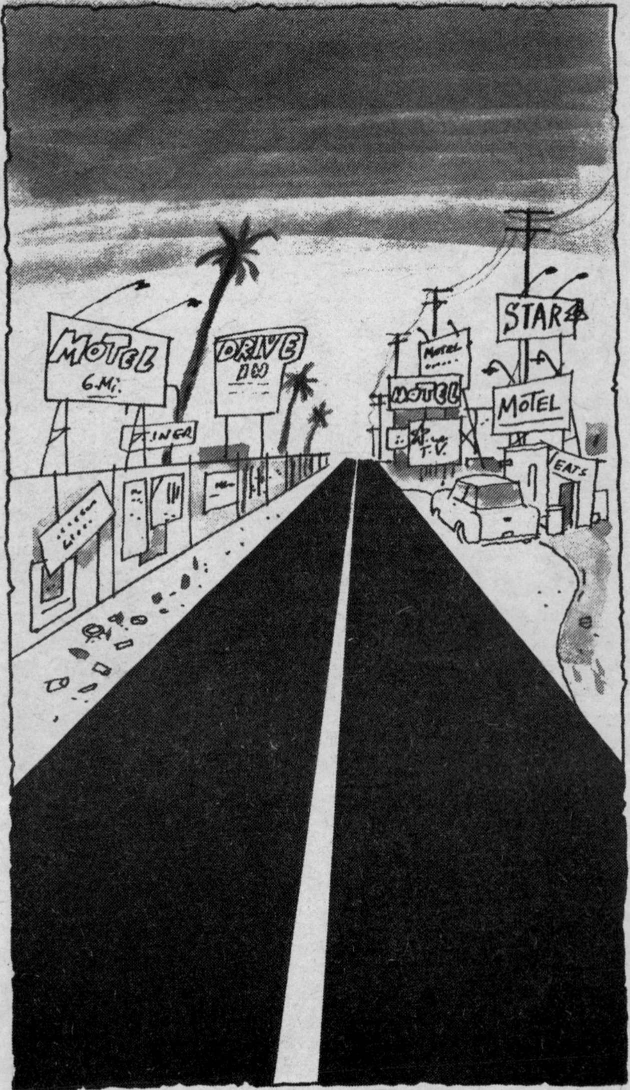
MOTEL
6 Mi.
DRIVE IN
STAR
MOTEL
MOTEL
MOTEL
T.V.
EATS

OUR FIRST STOP IN FLORIDA

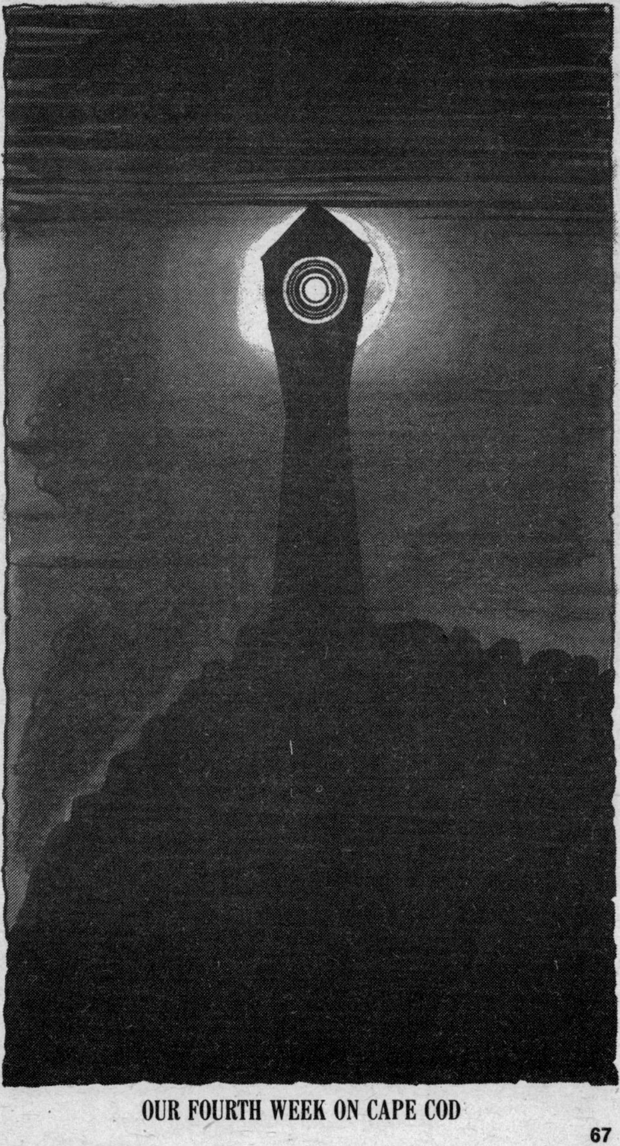

OUR FOURTH WEEK ON CAPE COD

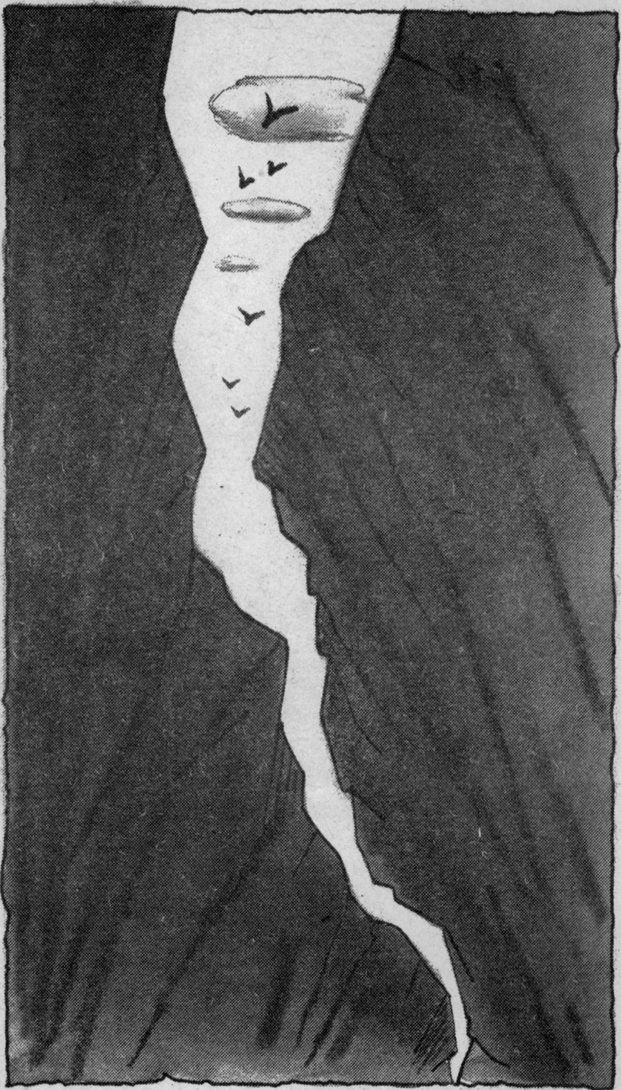

AT THE BOTTOM OF THE GRAND CANYON

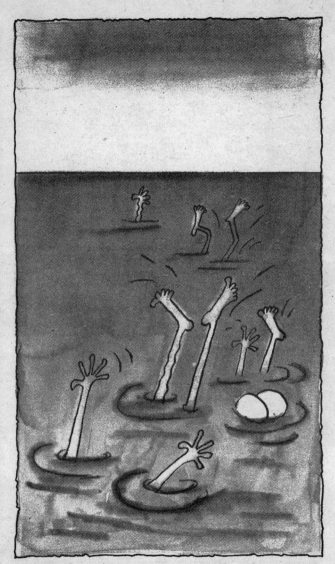

NATIVES DIVING FOR COINS

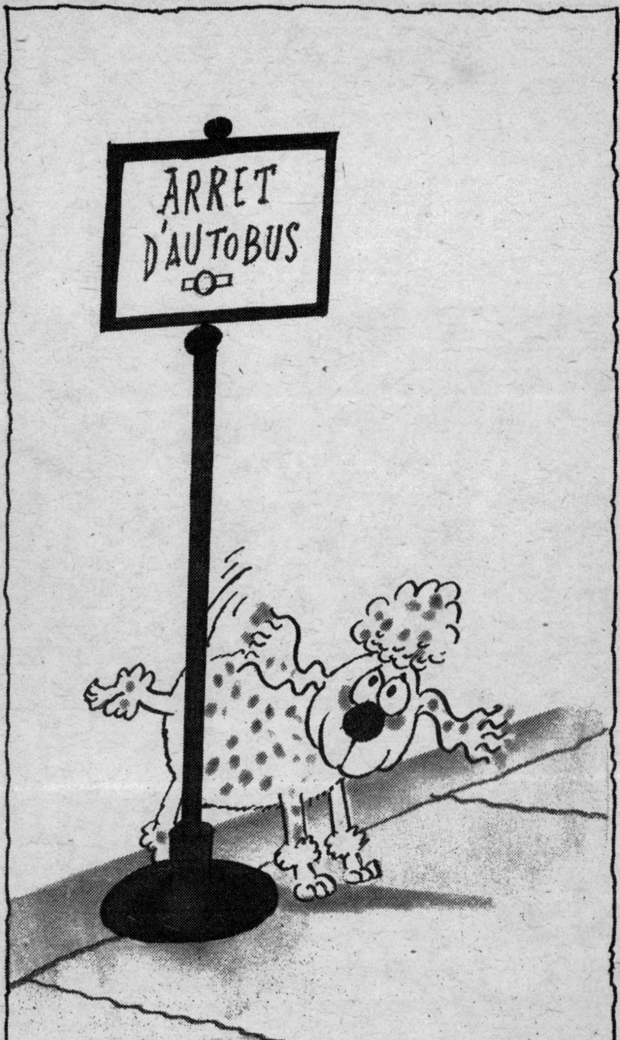
ARRET
D'AUTOBUS

A CUTE LITTLE FRENCH POODLE PUPPY

GROUP PHOTOS OF SOME NOT-SO-HISTORIC EVENTS

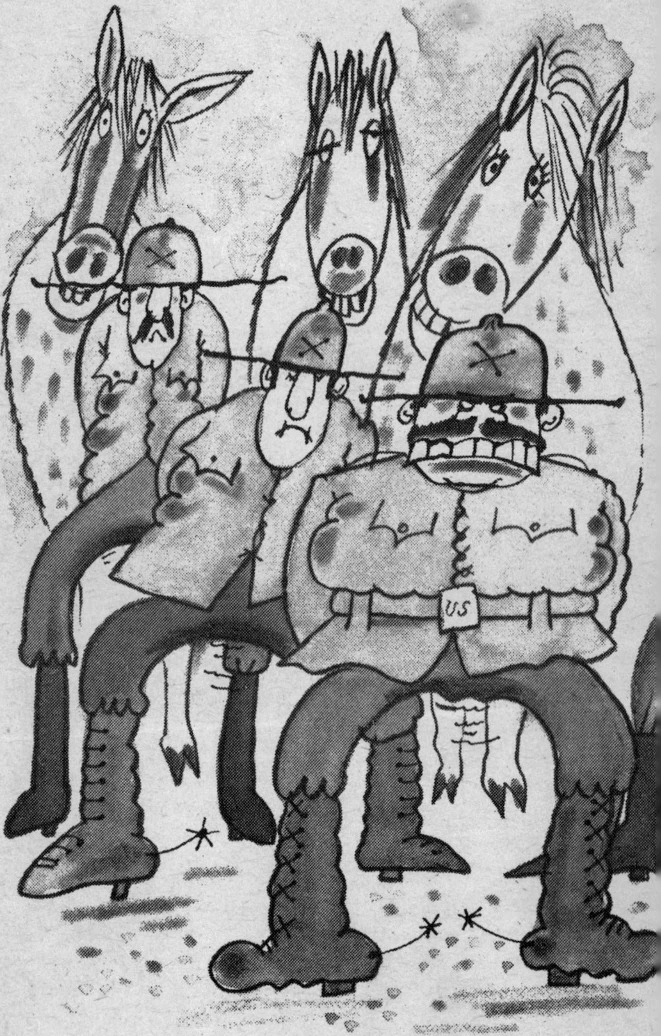
US

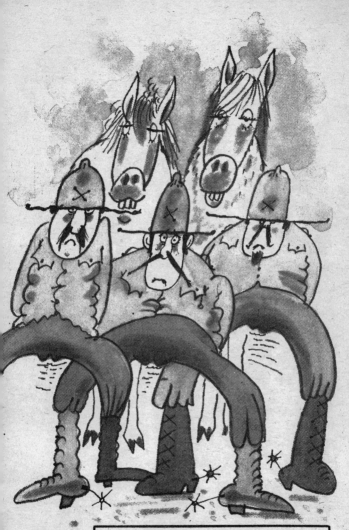

Teddy Roosevelt and the Rough Riders
after a rough day's ride

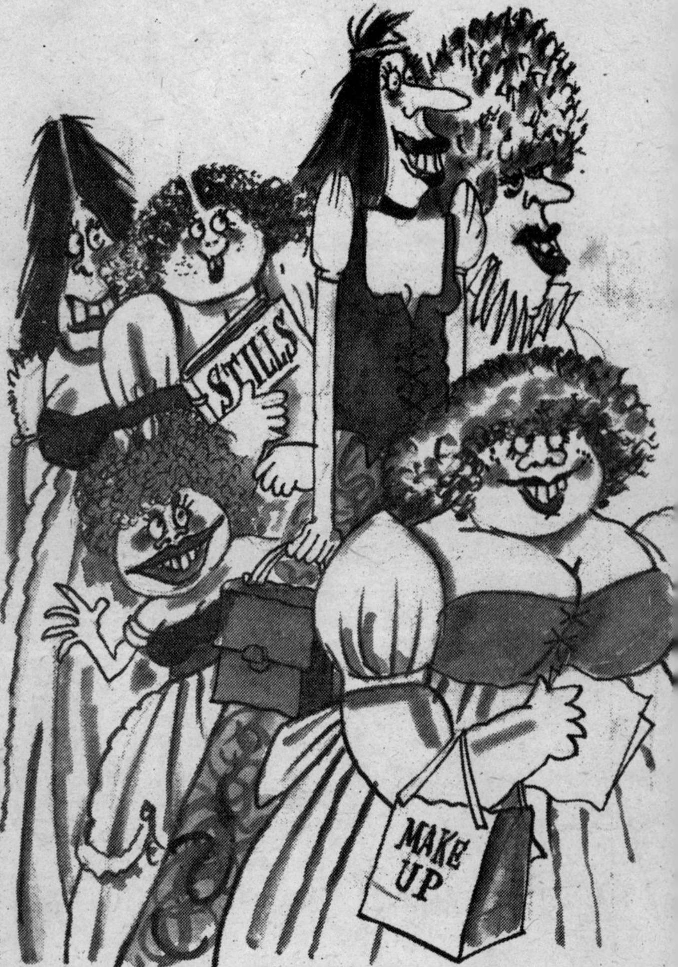
STILLS
MAKE UP

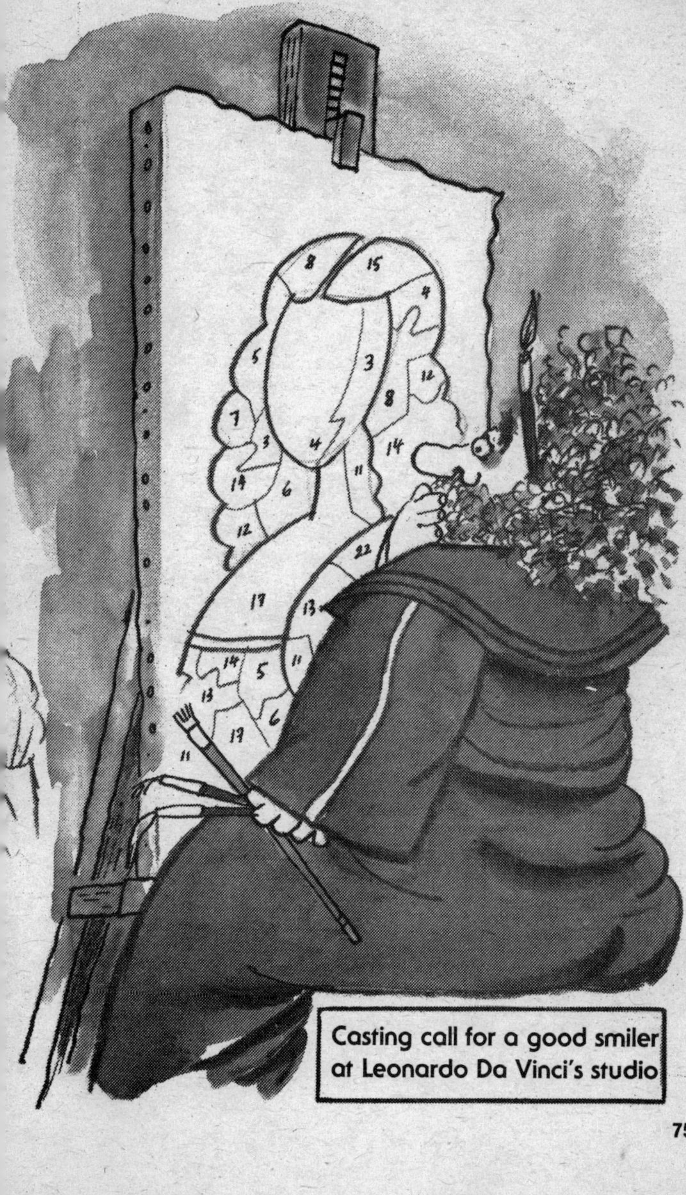

Casting call for a good smiler at Leonardo Da Vinci's studio

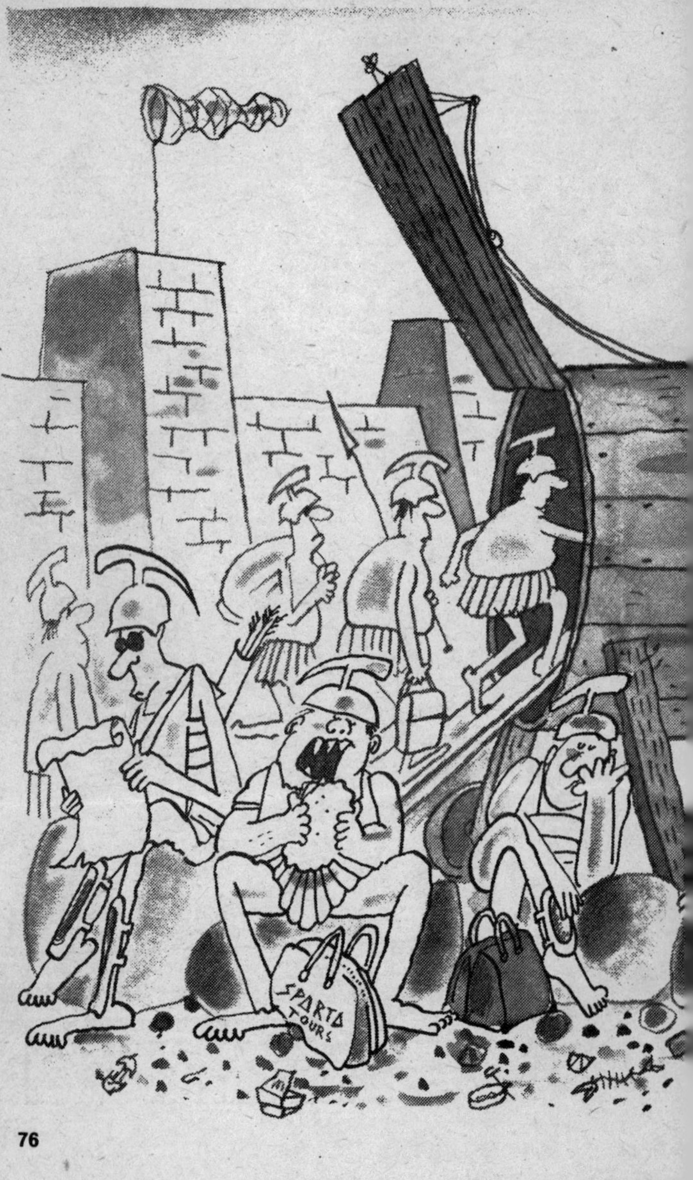
SPARTA TOURS

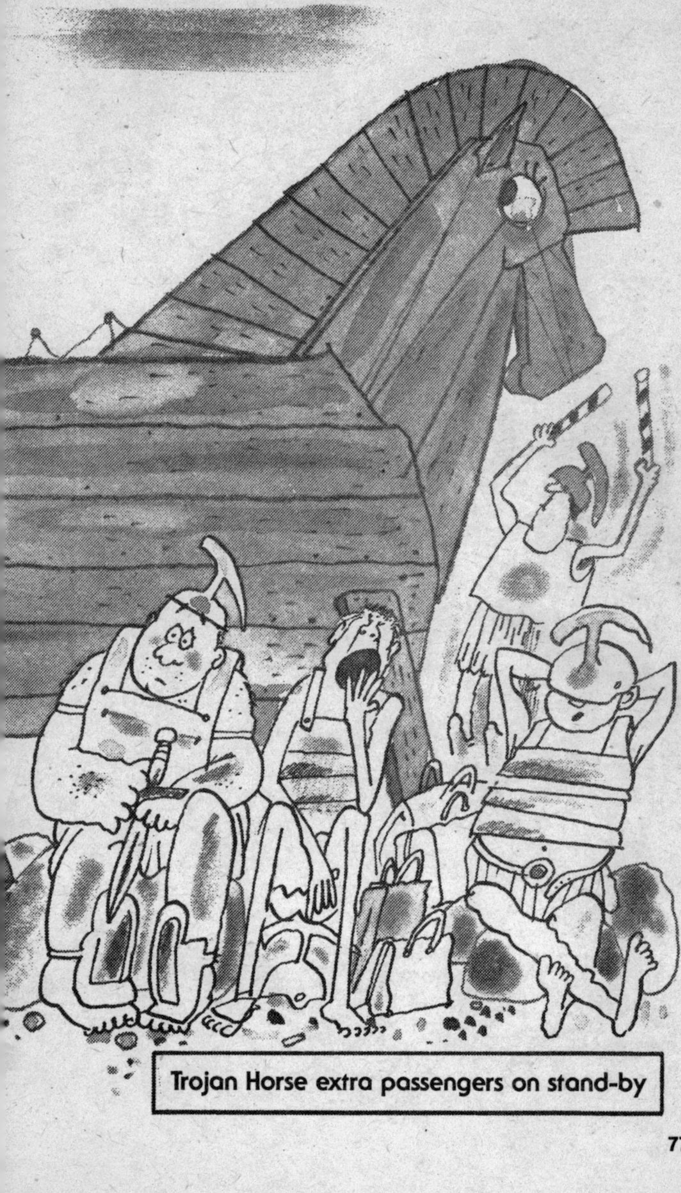

Trojan Horse extra passengers on stand-by

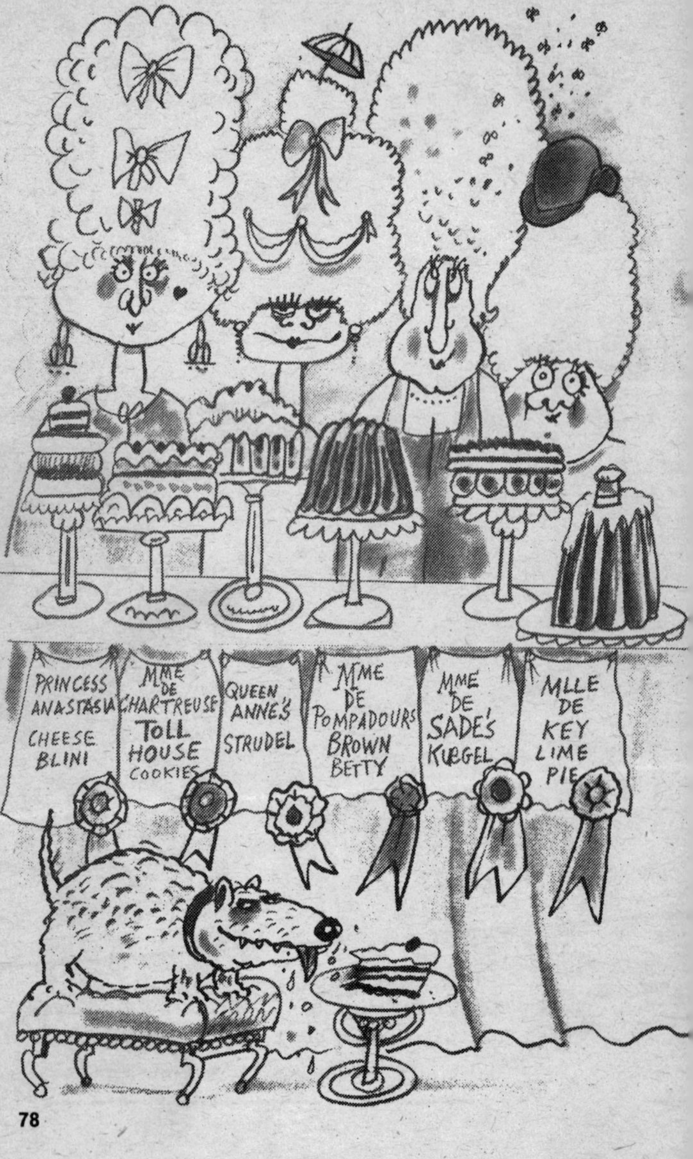
PRINCESS ANASTASIA CHEESE BLINI
Mme DE CHARTREUSE TOLL HOUSE COOKIES
QUEEN ANNE'S STRUDEL
Mme DE POMPADOUR'S BROWN BETTY
Mme DE SADE'S KUGEL
MLLE DE KEY LIME PIE

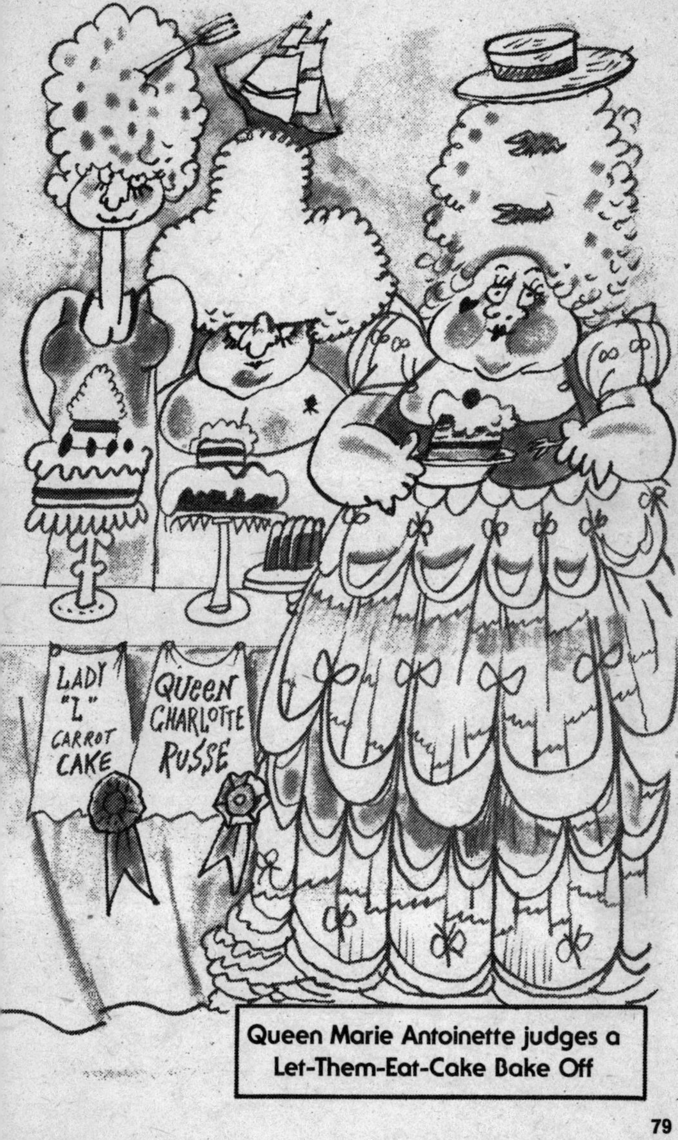
LADY
"L"
CARROT
CAKE
QUEEN
CHARLOTTE
RUSSE

Queen Marie Antoinette judges a
Let-Them-Eat-Cake Bake Off

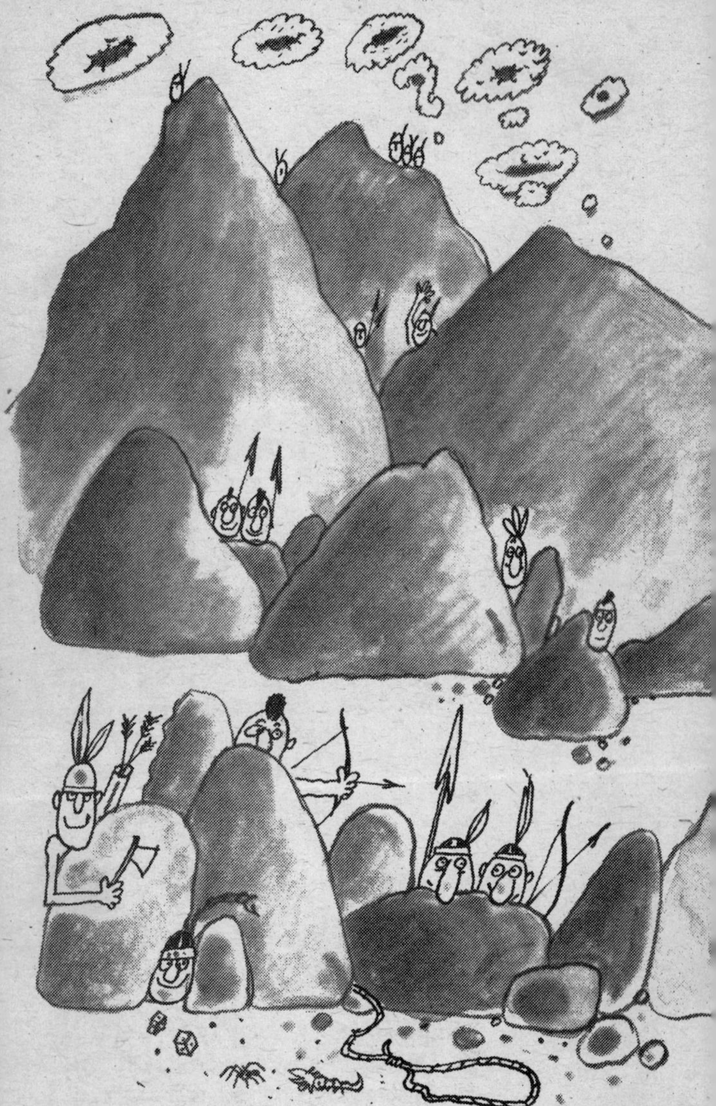

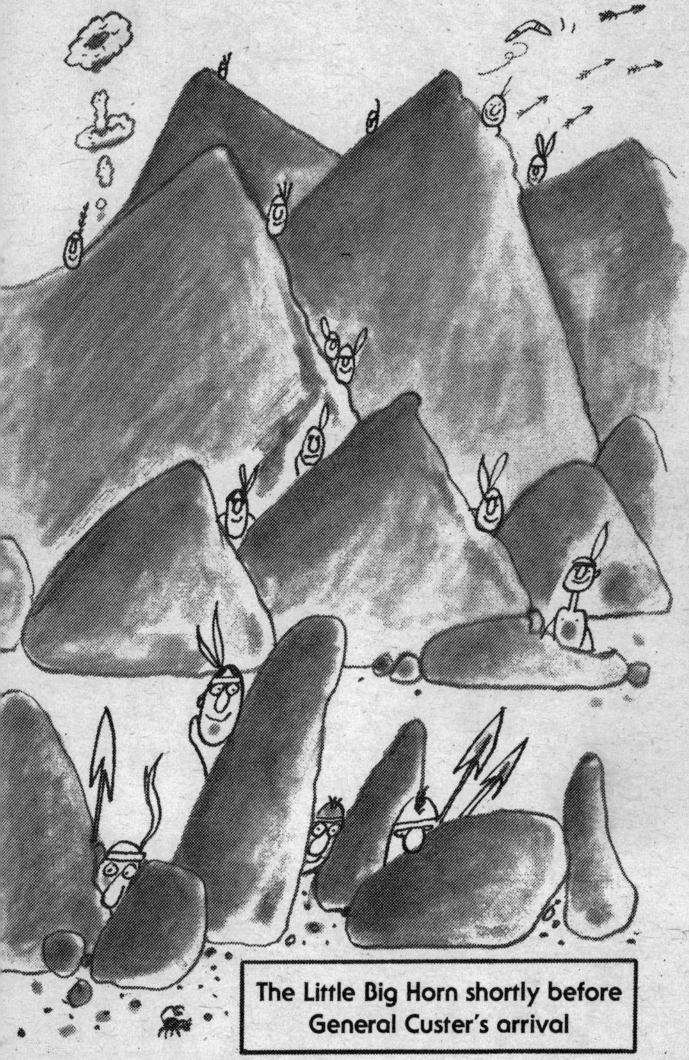

The Little Big Horn shortly before General Custer's arrival

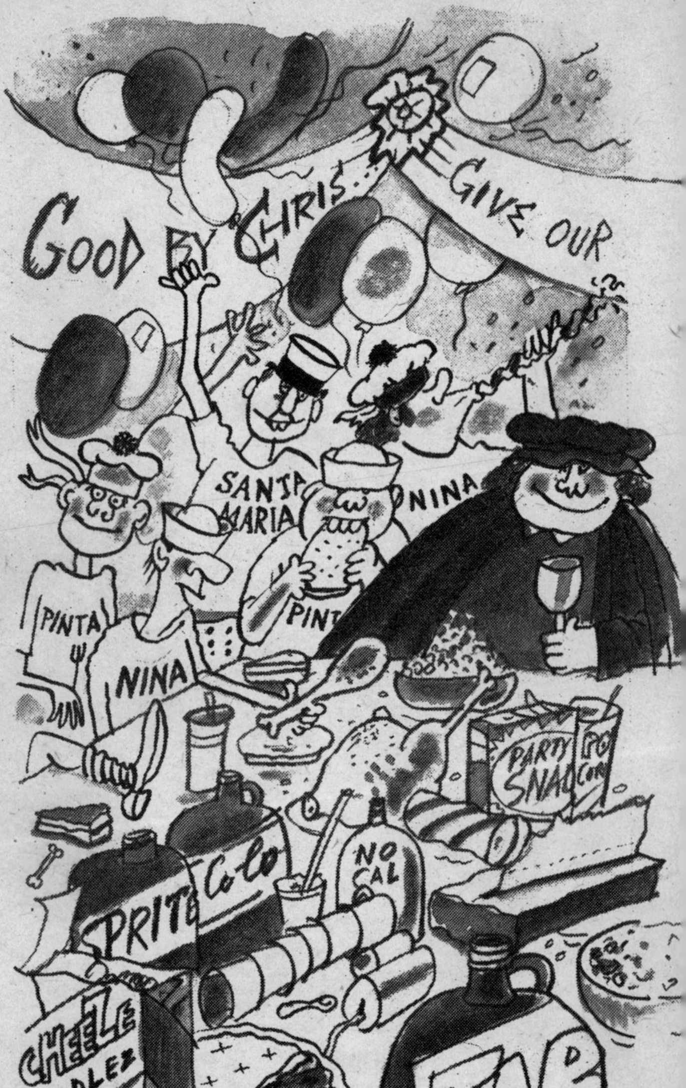
GOOD BY CHRIS... GIVE OUR
SANTA MARIA
NINA
PINTA
NINA
PINT
PARTY SNA
PO CORN
NO CAL
SPRITE
Co-Lo
CHEEZE OODLEZ

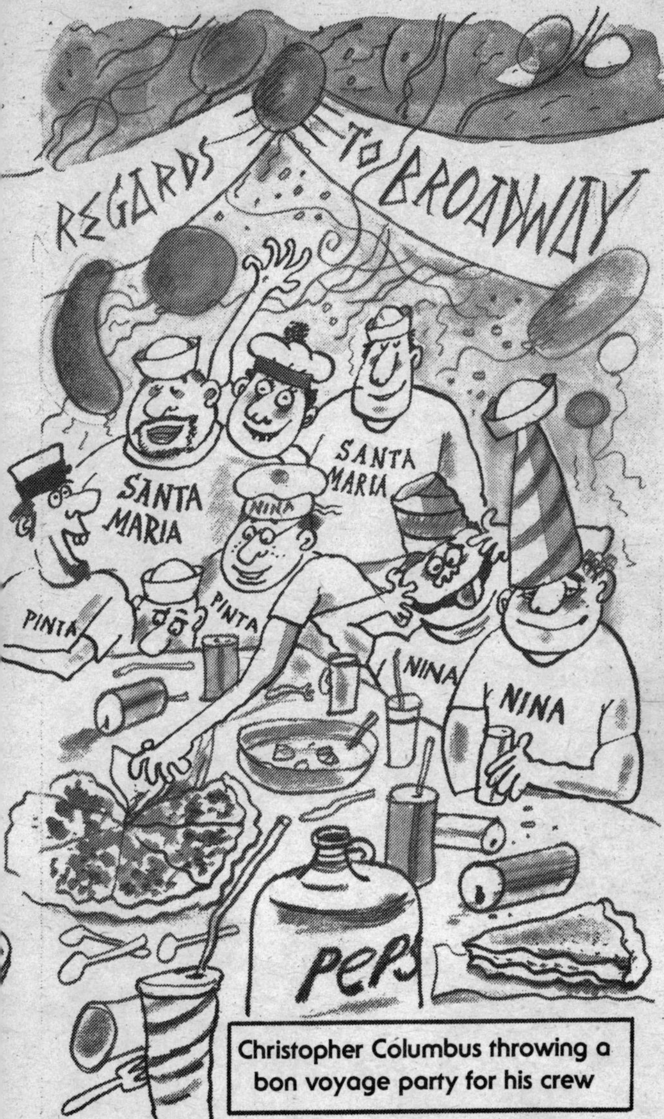
REGARDS TO BROADWAY
SANTA MARIA
SANTA MARIA
NINA
PINTA
PINTA
NINA
NINA
PEPS

Christopher Columbus throwing a bon voyage party for his crew

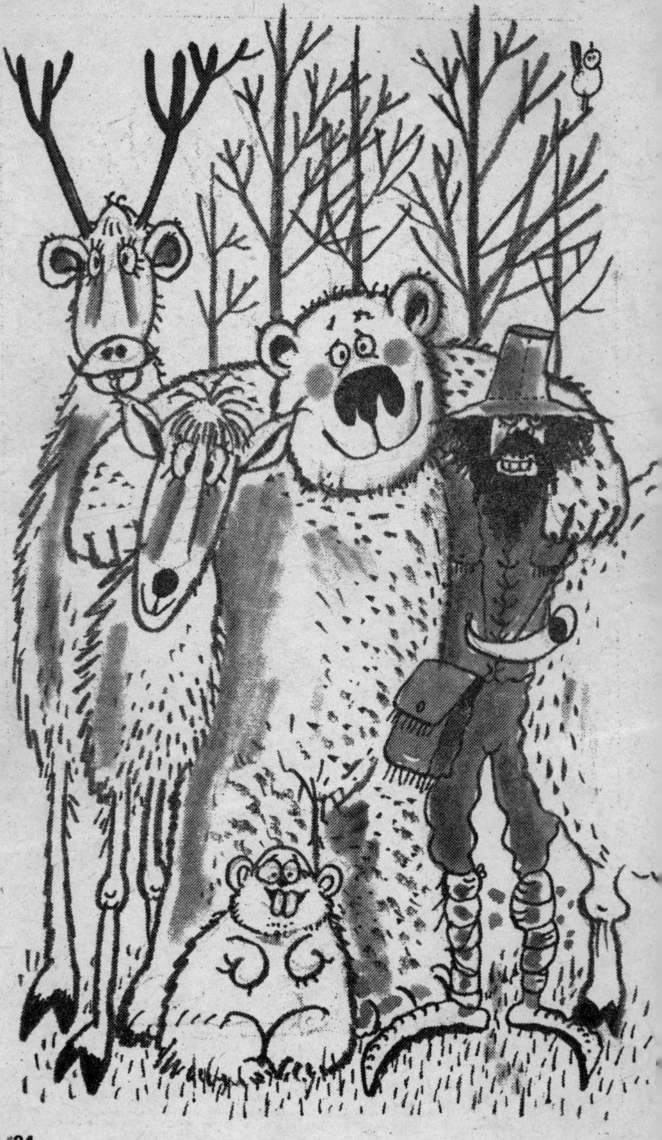

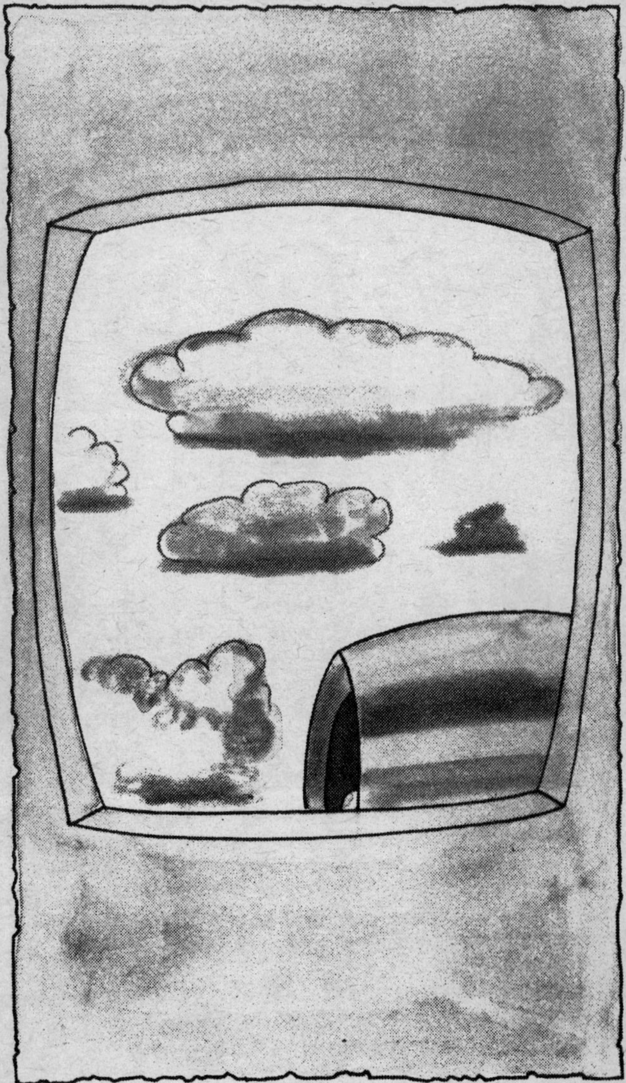

CROSSING THE EQUATOR AT 32,000 FEET

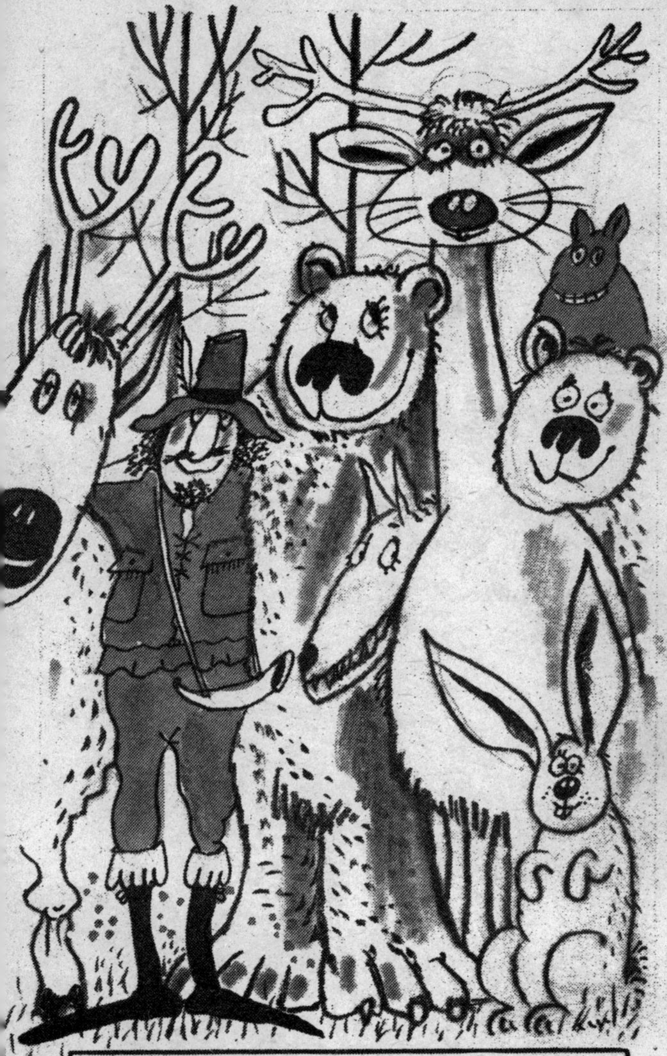

Lewis and Clark with a group of friendly locals

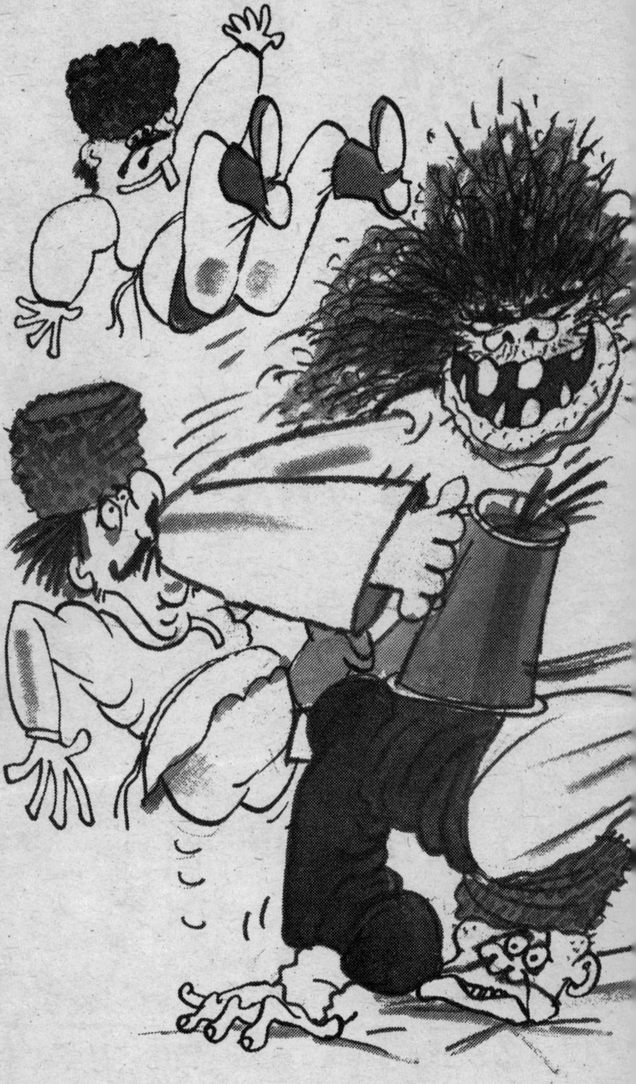

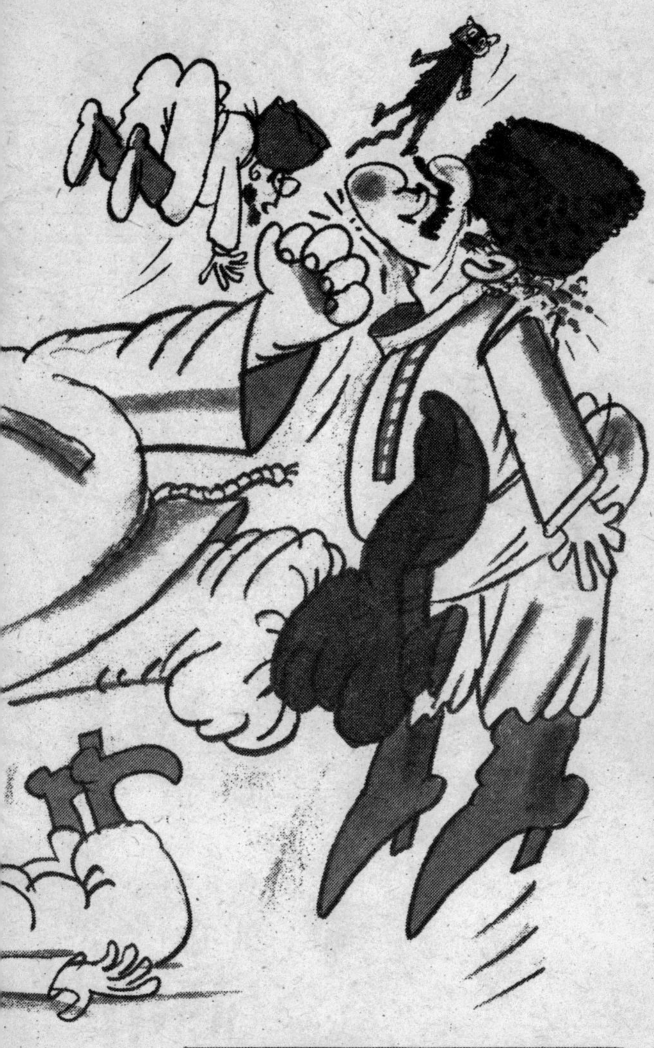

Ivan The Terrible having a good day

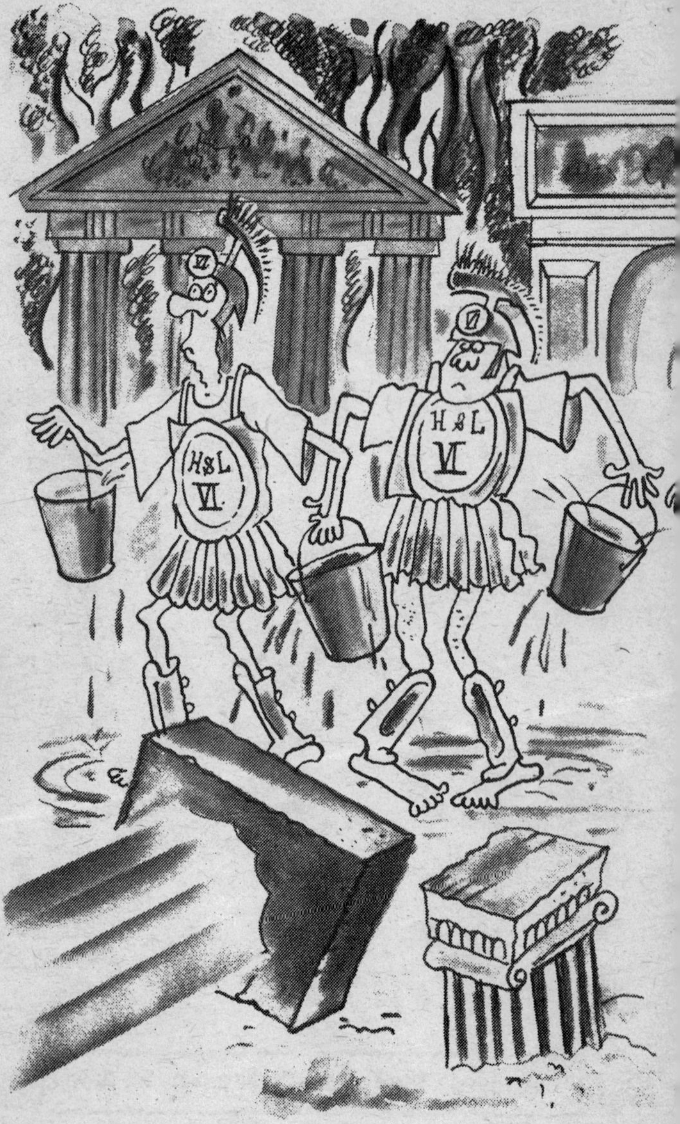
H&L
VI.
H&L
VI

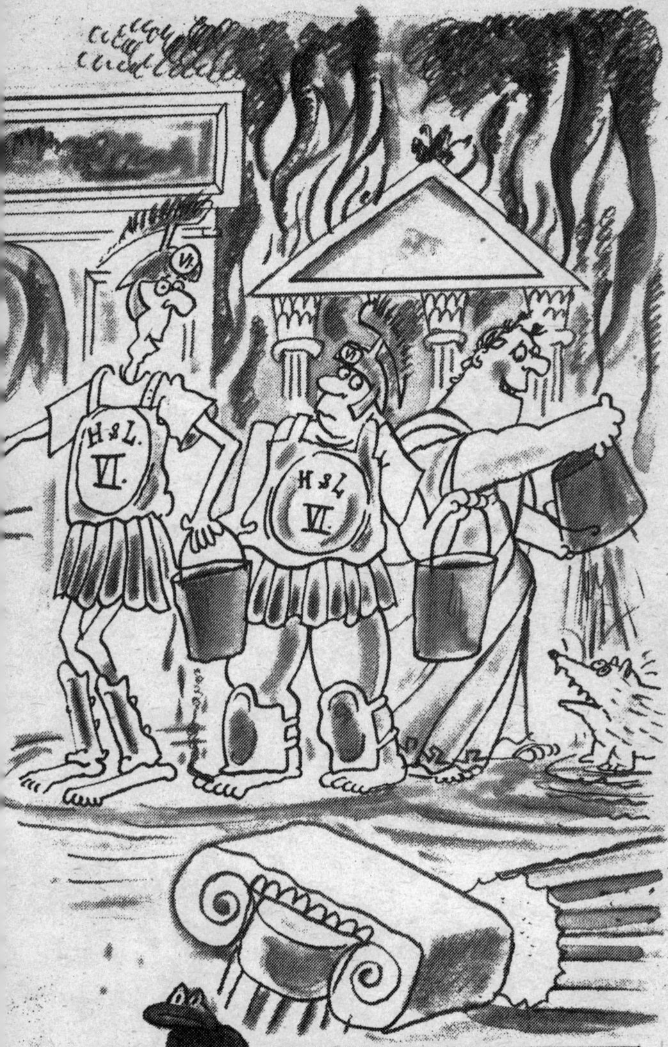
H&L.
VI.
H&L
VI.

The Emperor Nero with a Roman fire brigade

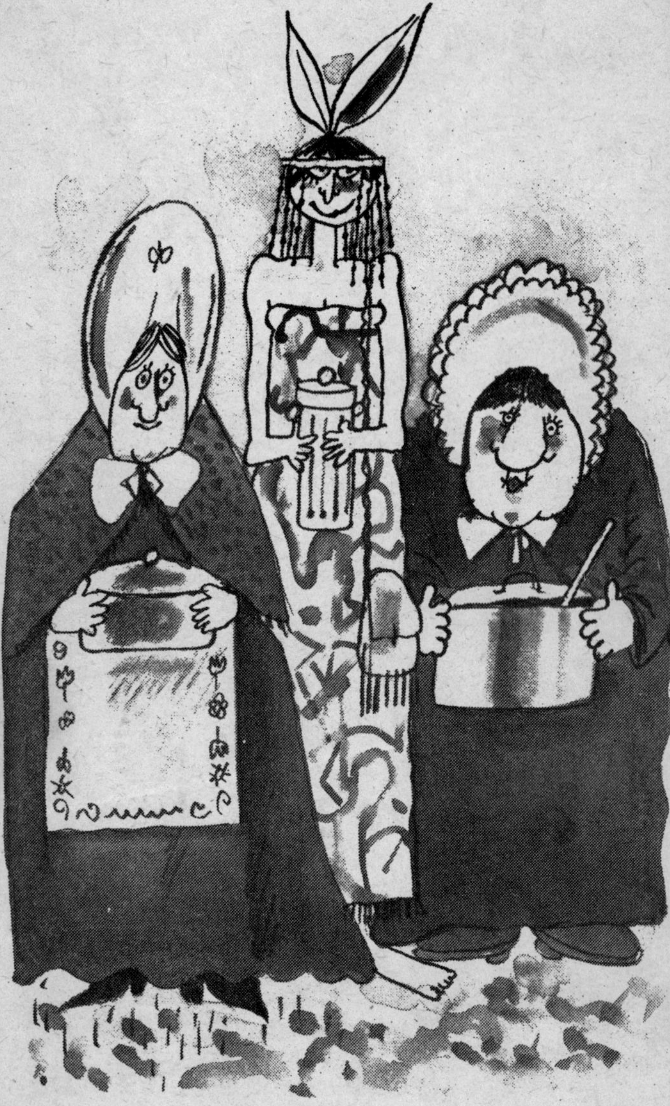

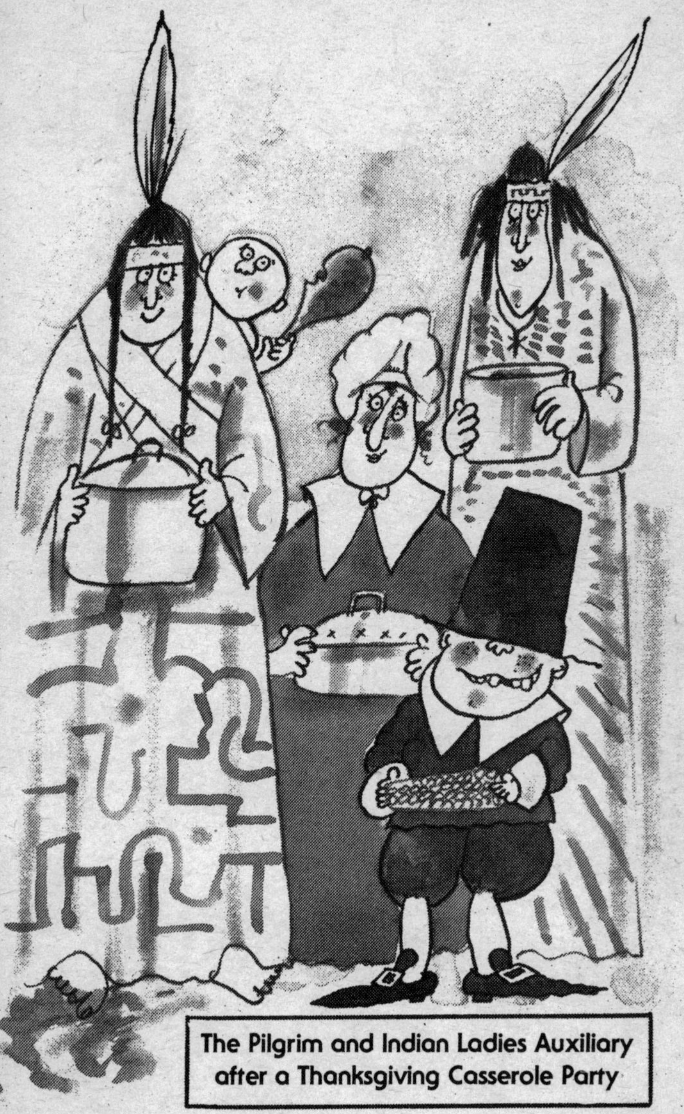

The Pilgrim and Indian Ladies Auxiliary
after a Thanksgiving Casserole Party

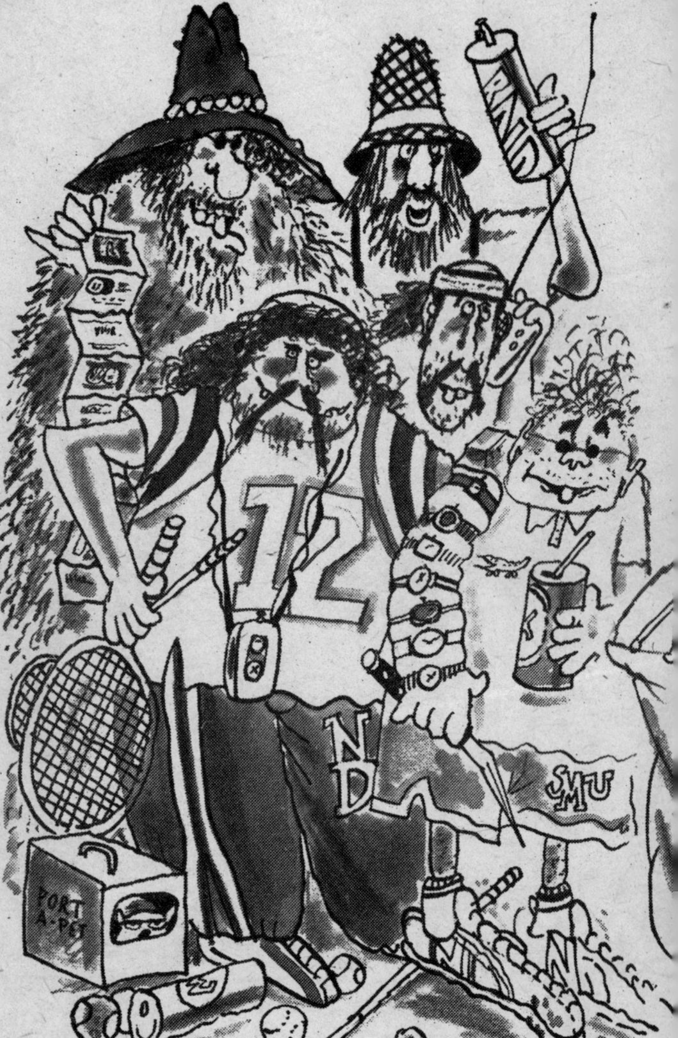
PORT
A-PET
SMU

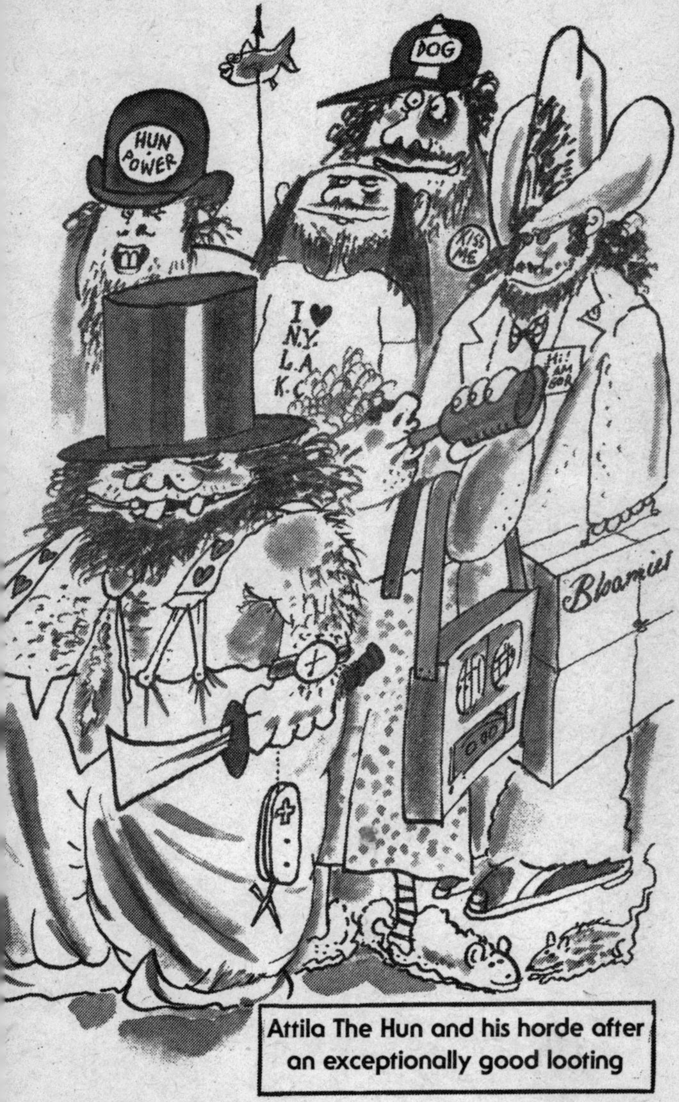
DOG
HUN · POWER
KISS ME
I ♥ N.Y. L.A. K.C.
Hi! I AM GOR
Bloomies

Attila The Hun and his horde after an exceptionally good looting

ON A CELEBRITY PHOTO HUNT

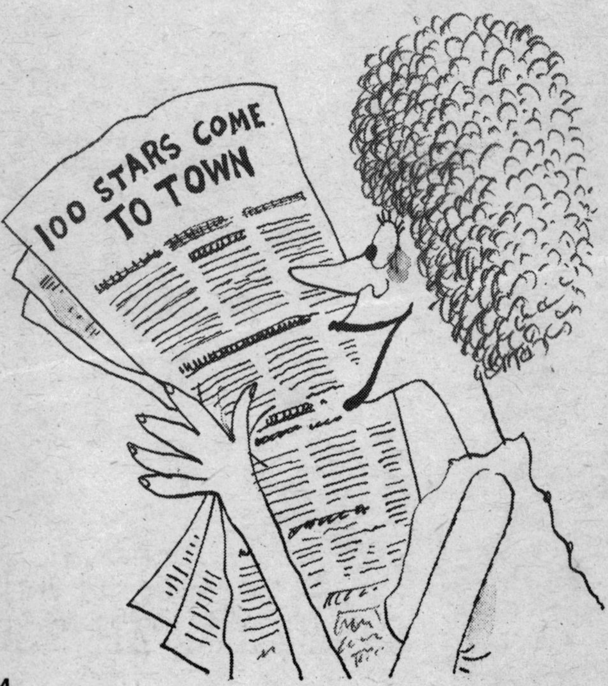
100 STARS COME TO TOWN

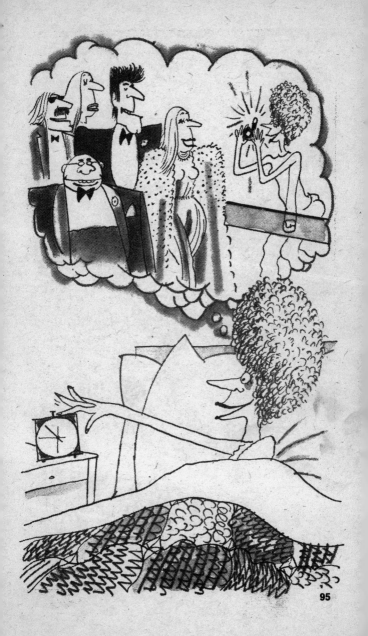

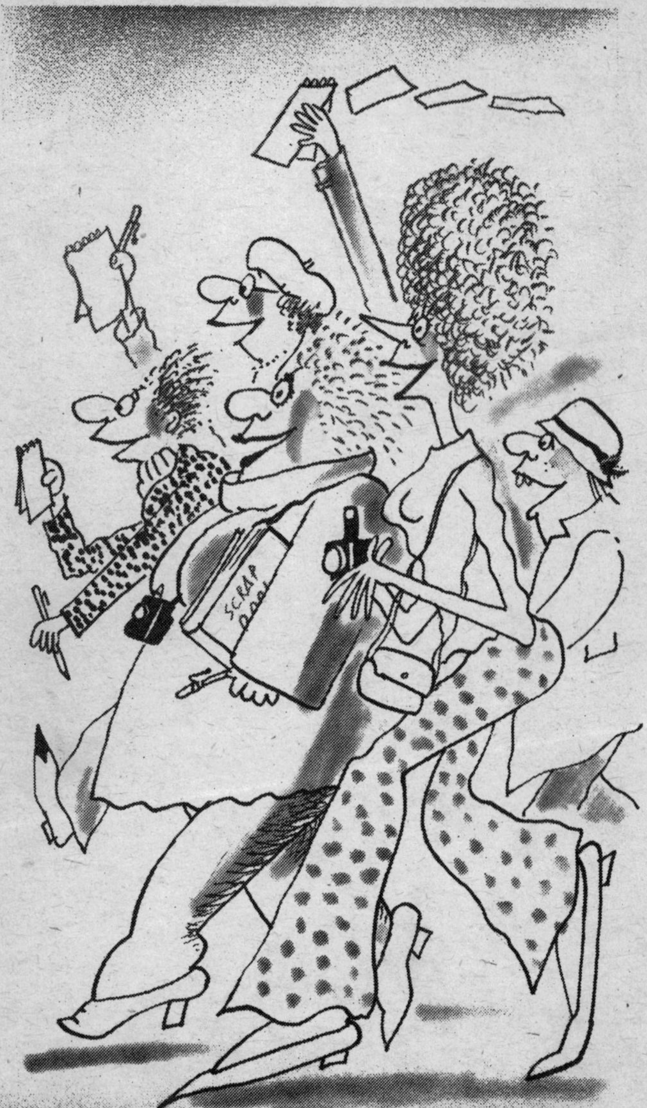
SCRAP

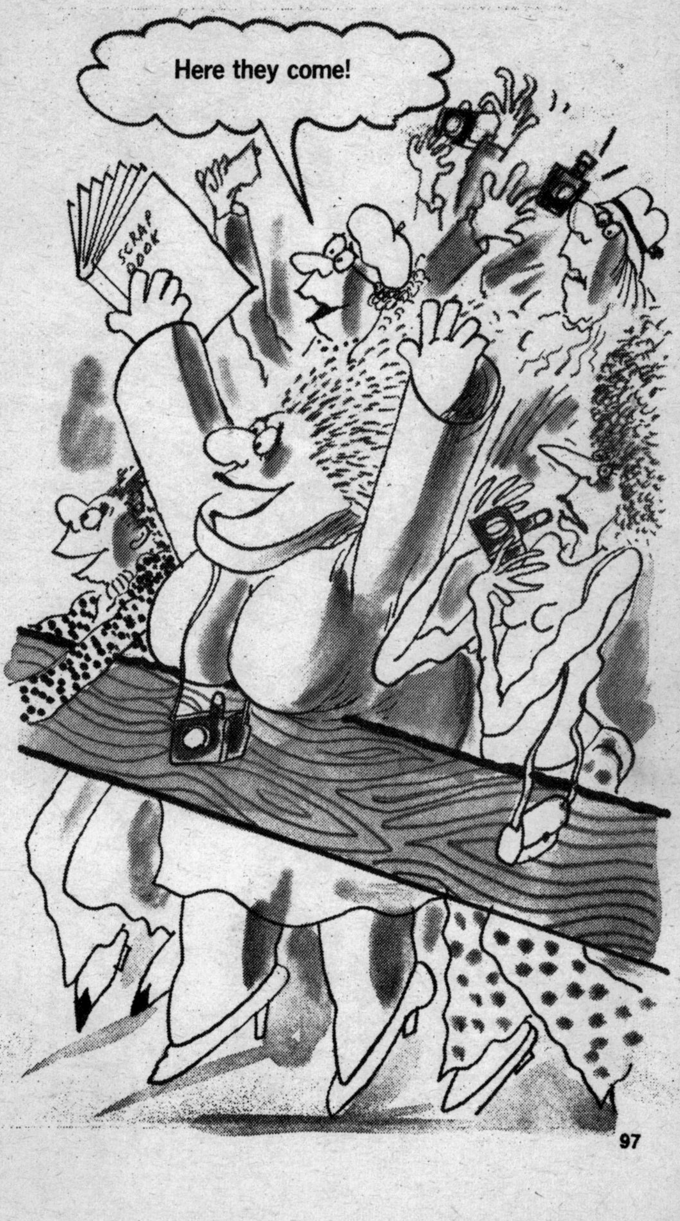
Here they come!
SCRAP BOOK

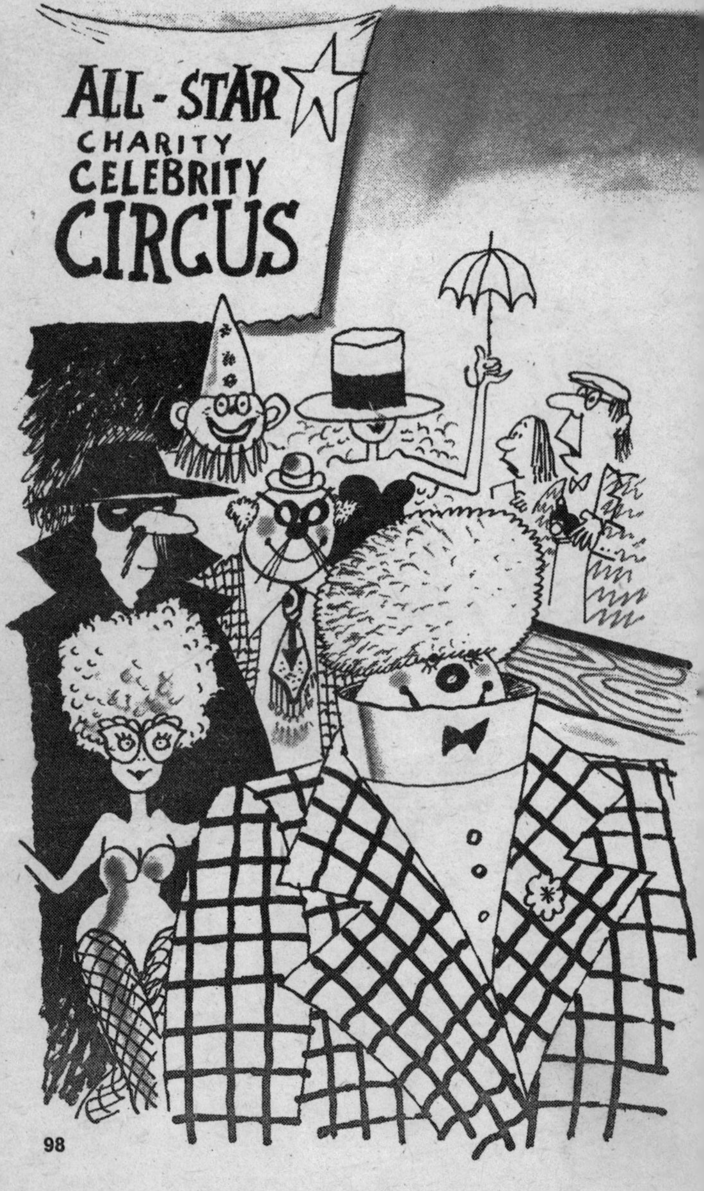
ALL-STAR
CHARITY
CELEBRITY
CIRCUS

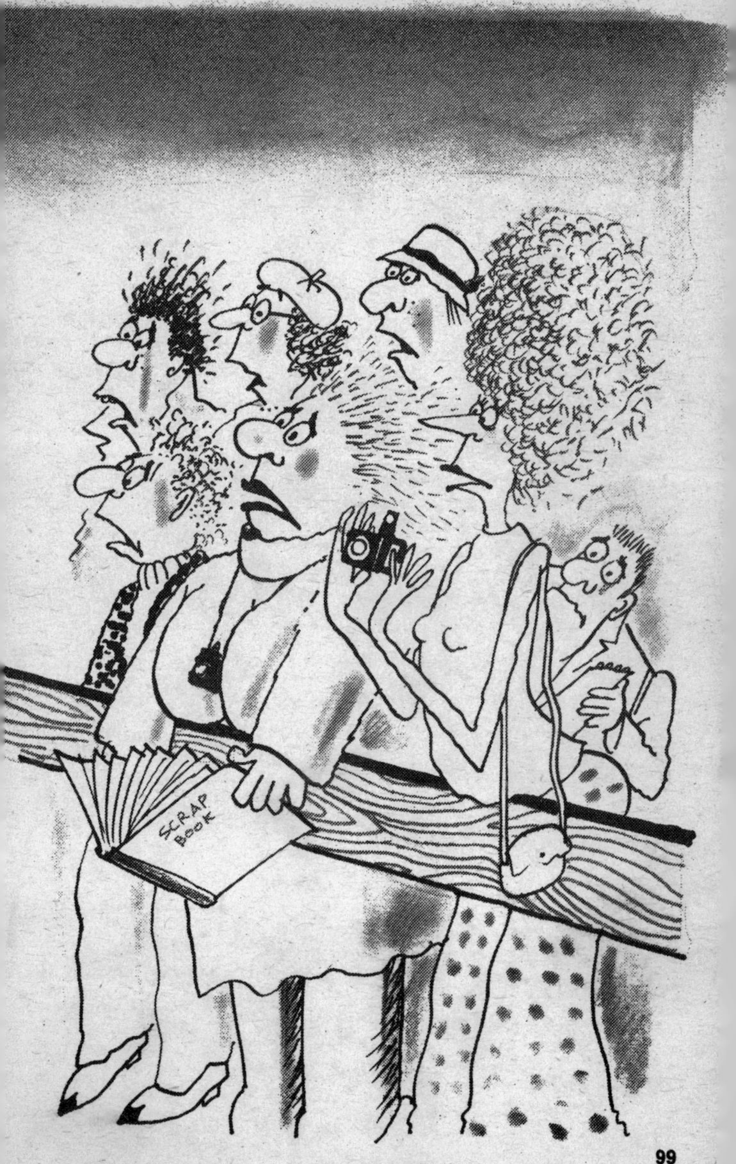
SCRAP BOOK

A COLLECTION
OF RARE
MAD
SATELLITE
PHOTOGRAPHS

RARE MAD SATELLITE PHOTOGRAPHS

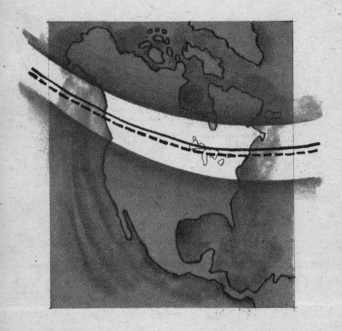

A WEST—EAST JET STREAM WITH NO PASSING
IN THE RIGHT LANE

RARE MAD SATELLITE PHOTOGRAPHS

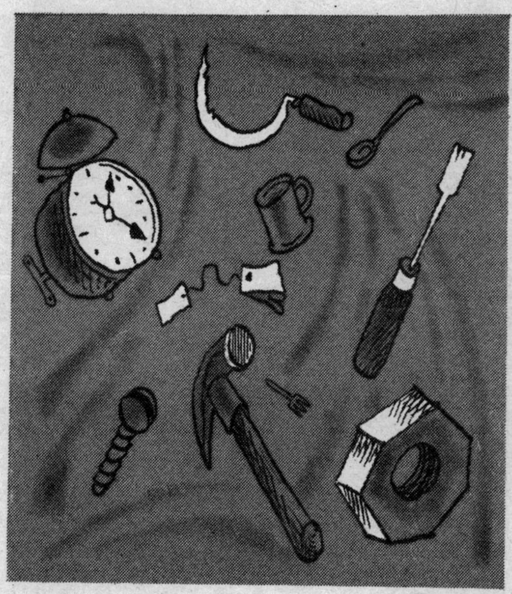

FREE-FLOATING SOVIET SPACESHIP
HARDWARE

RARE MAD SATELLITE PHOTOGRAPHS

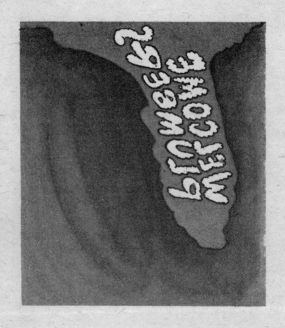

A SKYWRITER'S MESSAGE OVER THE MIAMI
CONVENTION CENTER

RARE MAD SATELLITE PHOTOGRAPHS

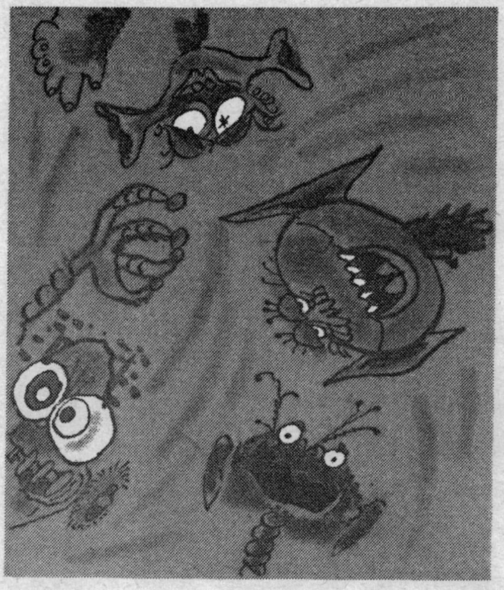

U.F.O.'S MUGGING FOR THE CAMERA

RARE MAD SATELLITE PHOTOGRAPHS

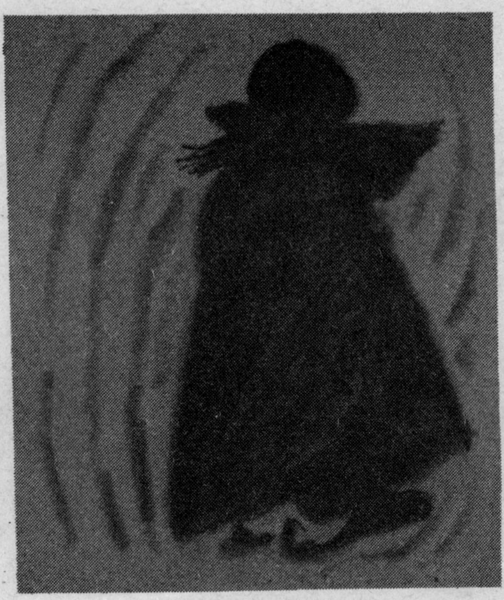

A MID-ATLANTIC OIL SLICK

RARE MAD SATELLITE PHOTOGRAPHS

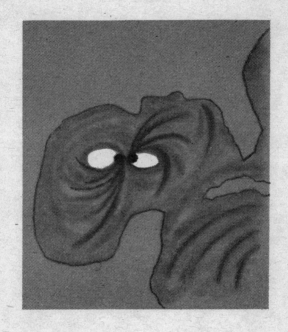

HURRICANES ALBERT AND BERTHA CROSSING EYES IN THE GULF OF MEXICO

RARE MAD SATELLITE PHOTOGRAPHS

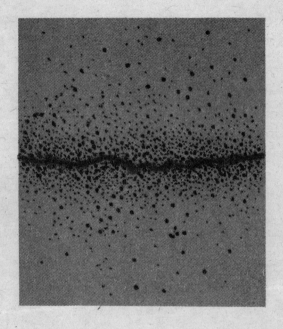

THE GRAND CANYON AT THE HEIGHT OF THE TOURIST SEASON

RARE MAD SATELLITE PHOTOGRAPHS

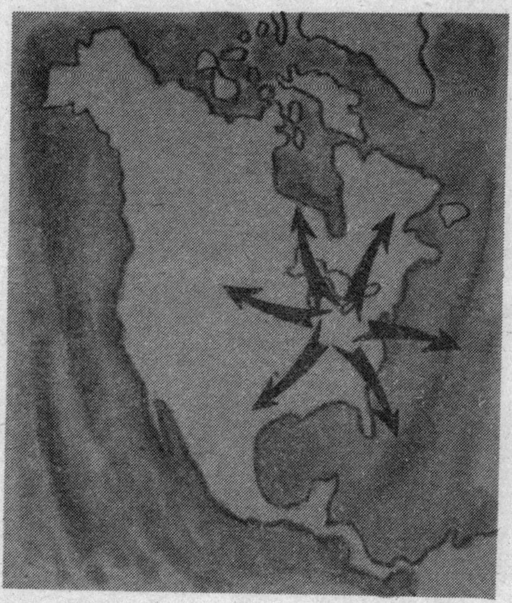

THE DAY OHIO HAD NO WEATHER

RARE MAD SATELLITE PHOTOGRAPHS

SEVERAL LOOSE SPACESHIP HEAT TILES AND
AN ASTRONAUT'S PEANUT AND JELLY SANDWICH

RARE MAD SATELLITE PHOTOGRAPHS

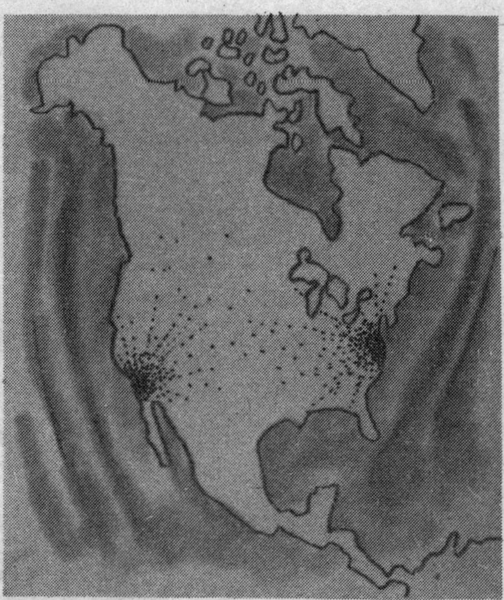

SIMULTANEOUS GRIDLOCKS ON THE NEW JERSEY TURNPIKE AND SAN DIEGO FREEWAY

THE
MAD
CENSORED
FAMILY
PHOTO
ALBUM

Big sis B***y after her second Weight Watcher's meeting

Cousin W***y's short-lived boxing career

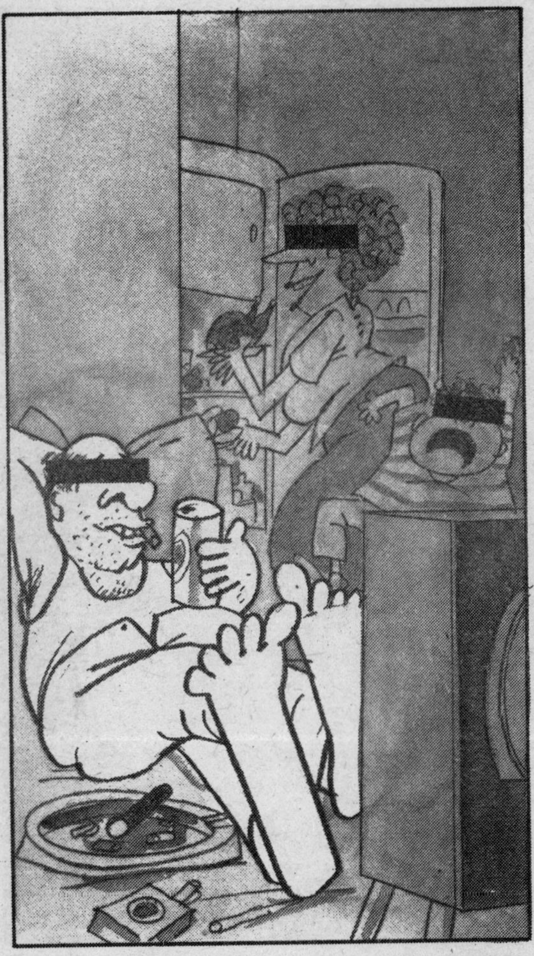

Our visiting relatives from O**o after twenty-three days

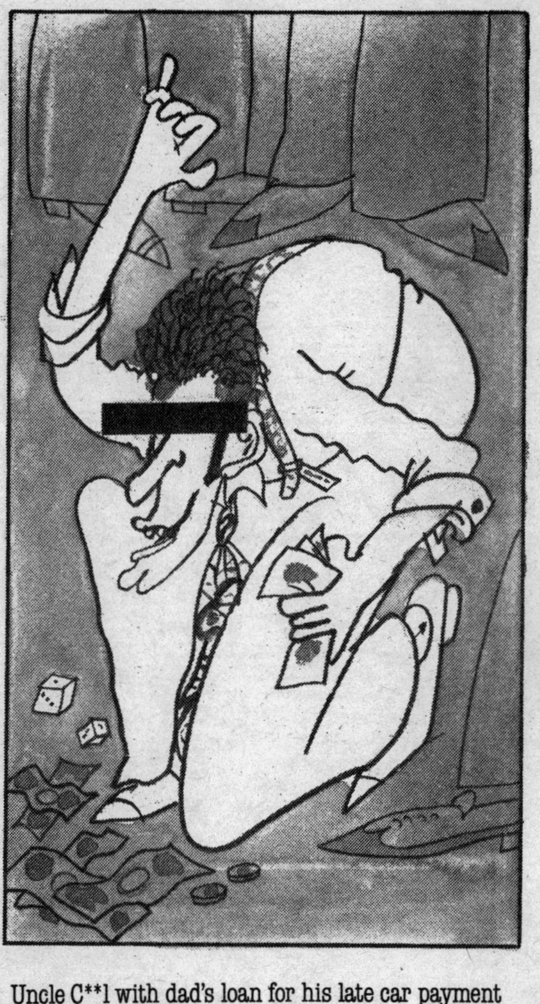

Uncle C**l with dad's loan for his late car payment

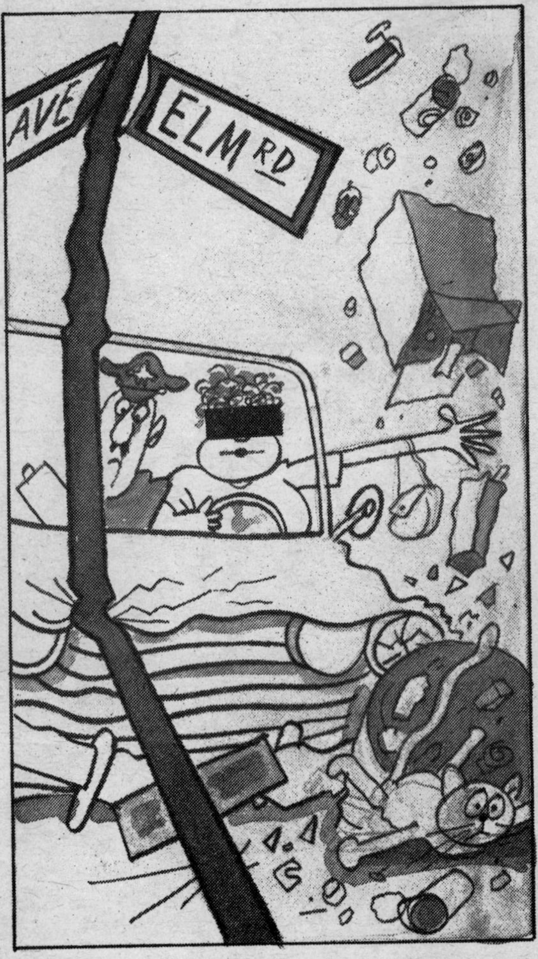
AVE
ELM RD

Mom's ***th attempt to pass her driver's test

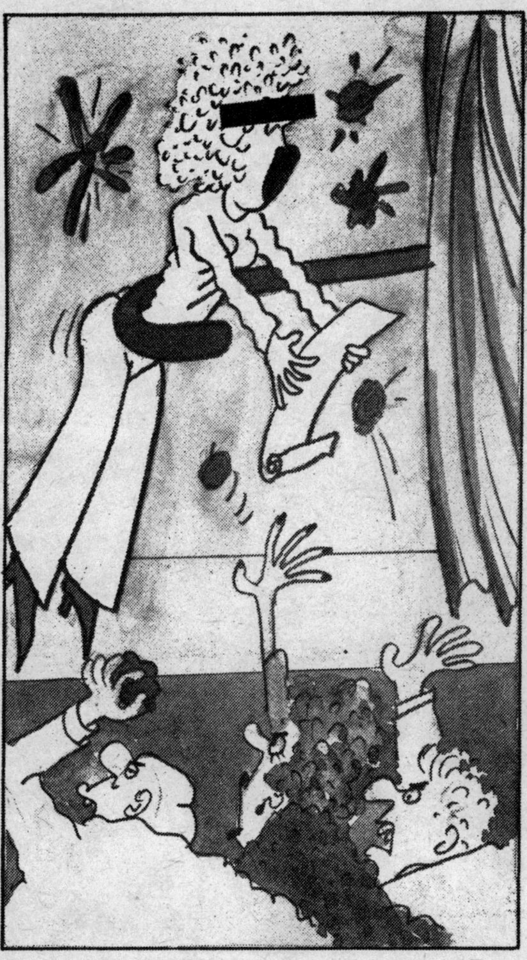

Aunt L**y's short-lived show-biz career

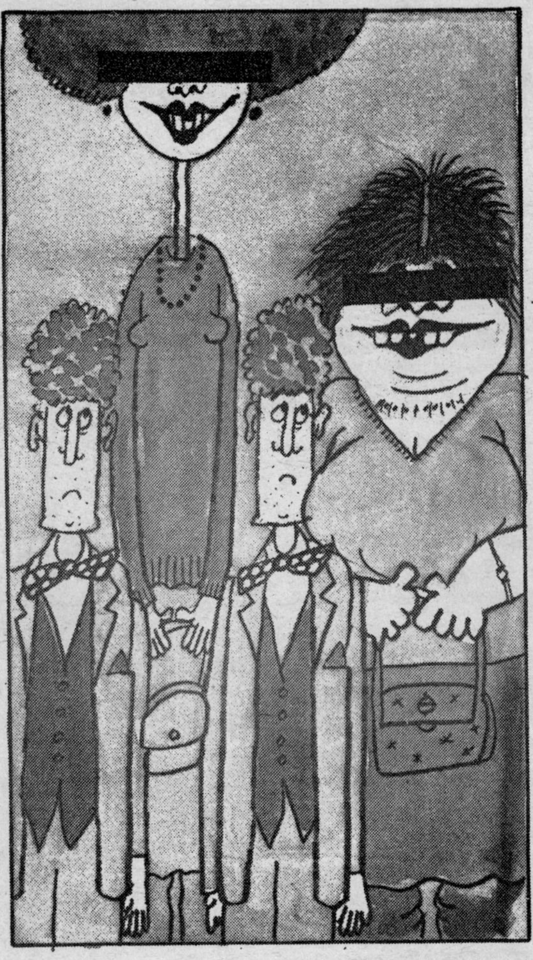

Our twins and their blind dates, the P*****y sisters

Dad's Fraternity Brothers—
Now: Senator K****t, Judge M****y, Lawyers
B****s and W*******t and Doctor R****y

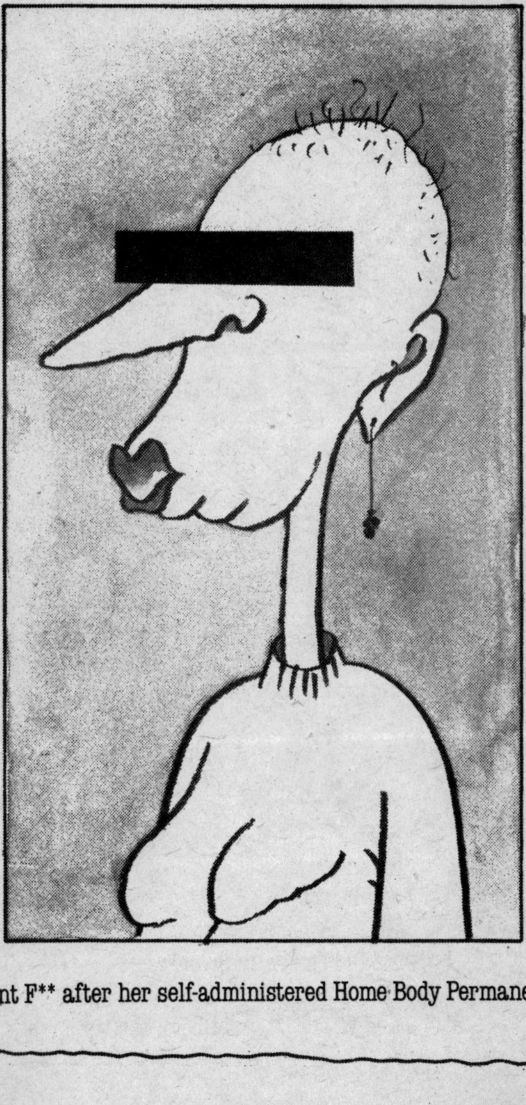

Aunt F** after her self-administered Home Body Permanent

FOTO FIRSTS!

First time appearing on stage

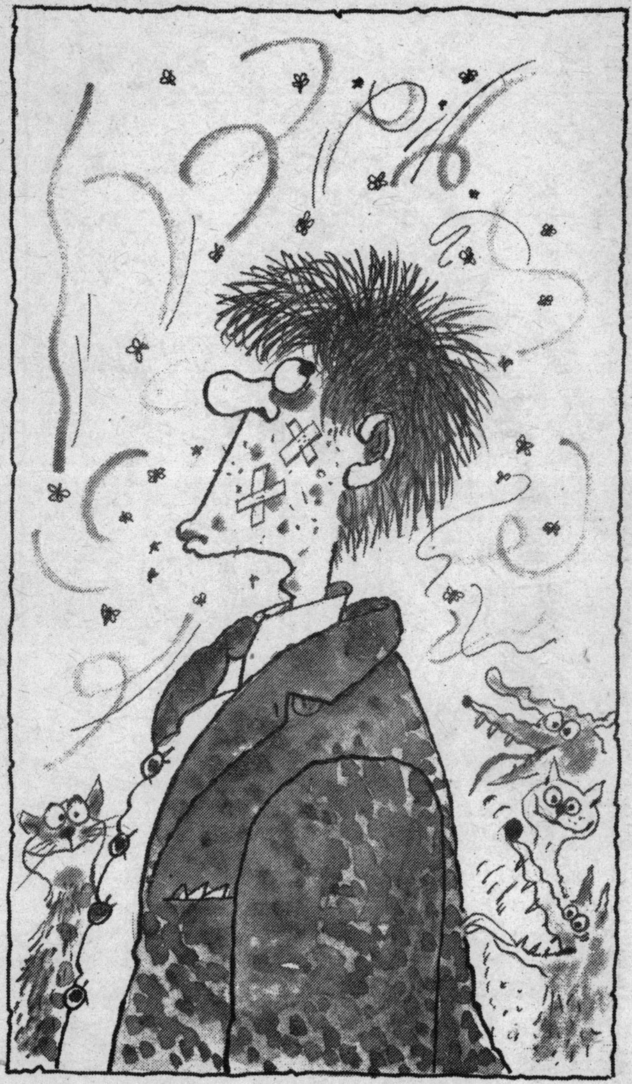

First time using after shave lotion

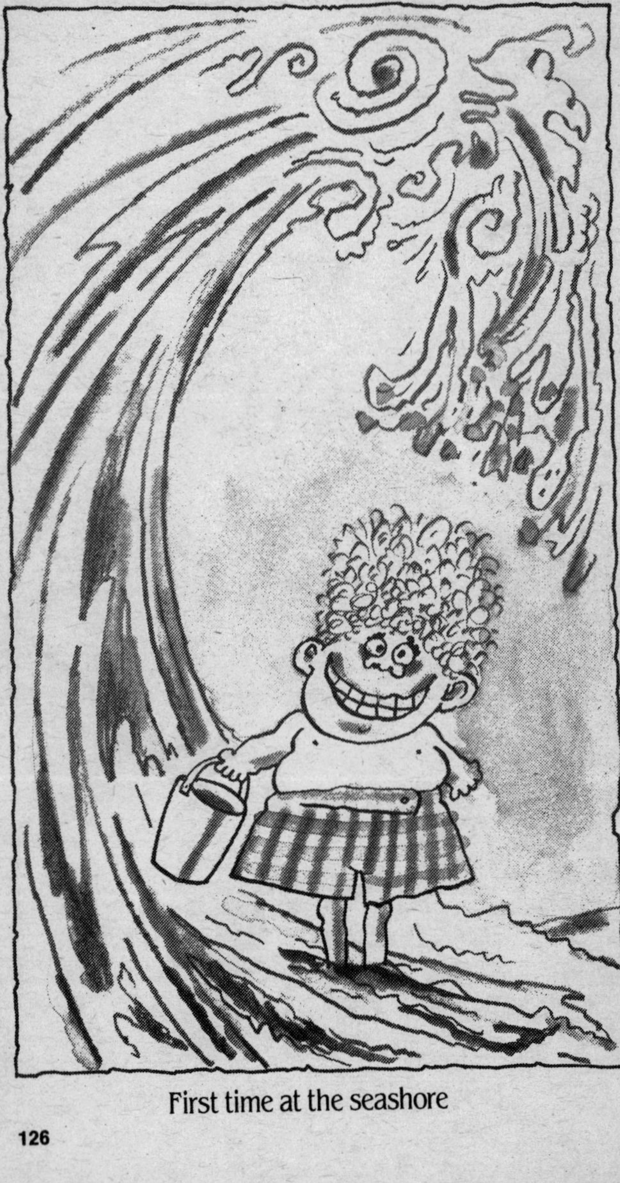

First time at the seashore

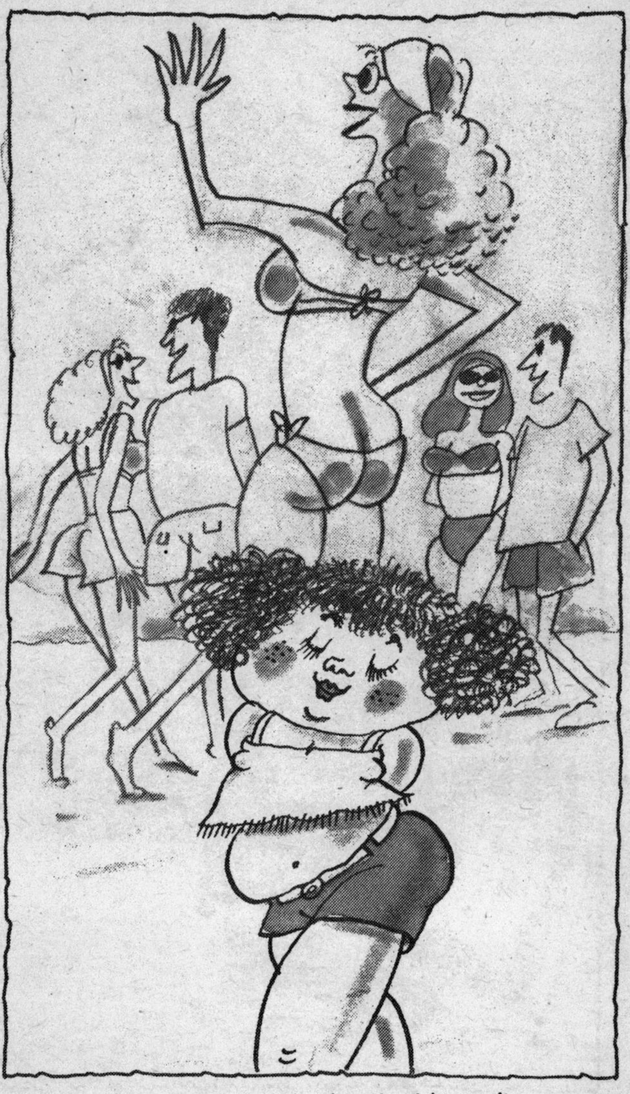

First time in a two piece bathing suit

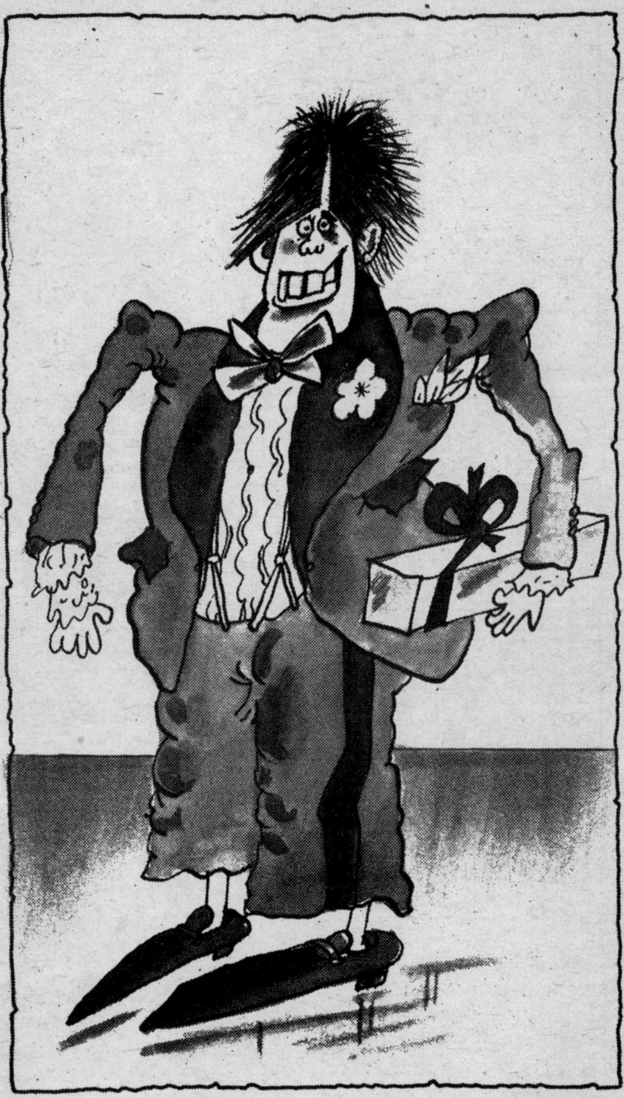

First time in a rented tuxedo

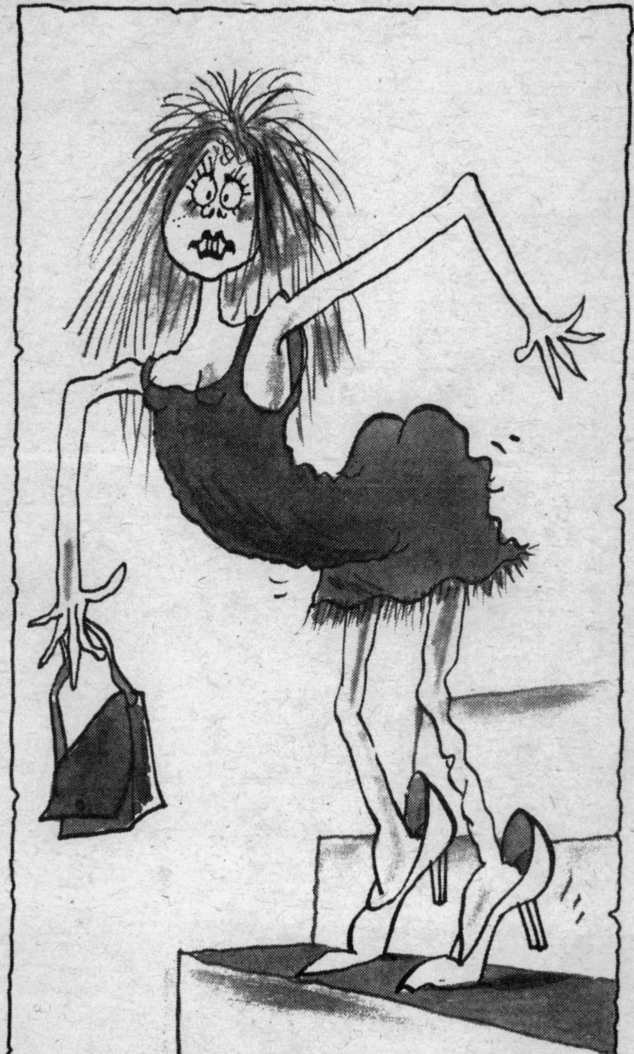

First time in high heels

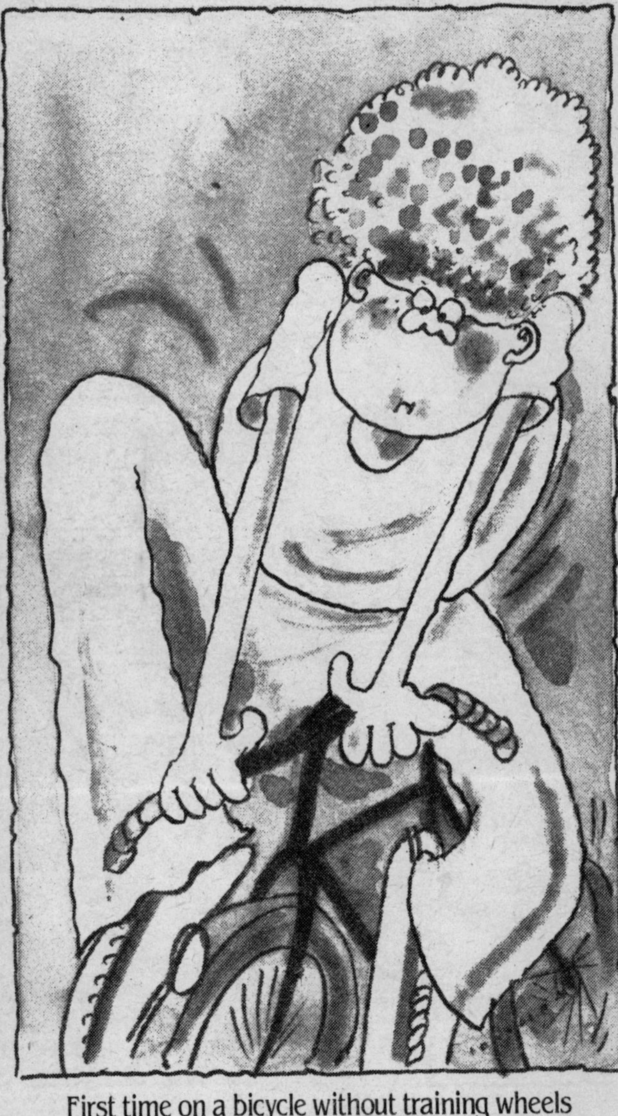

First time on a bicycle without training wheels

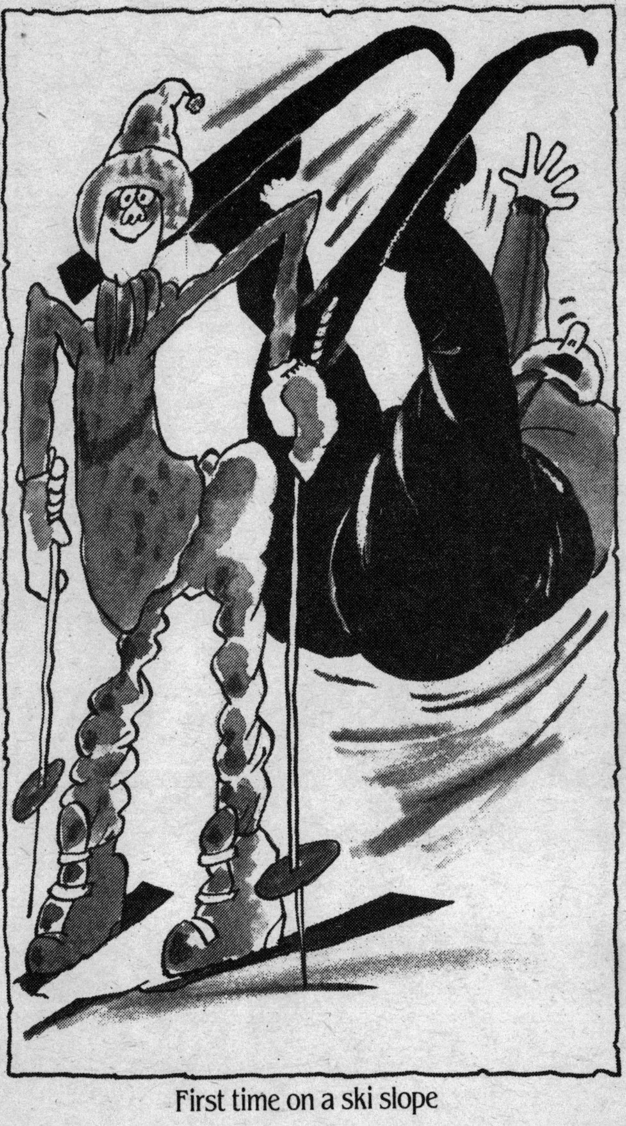

First time on a ski slope

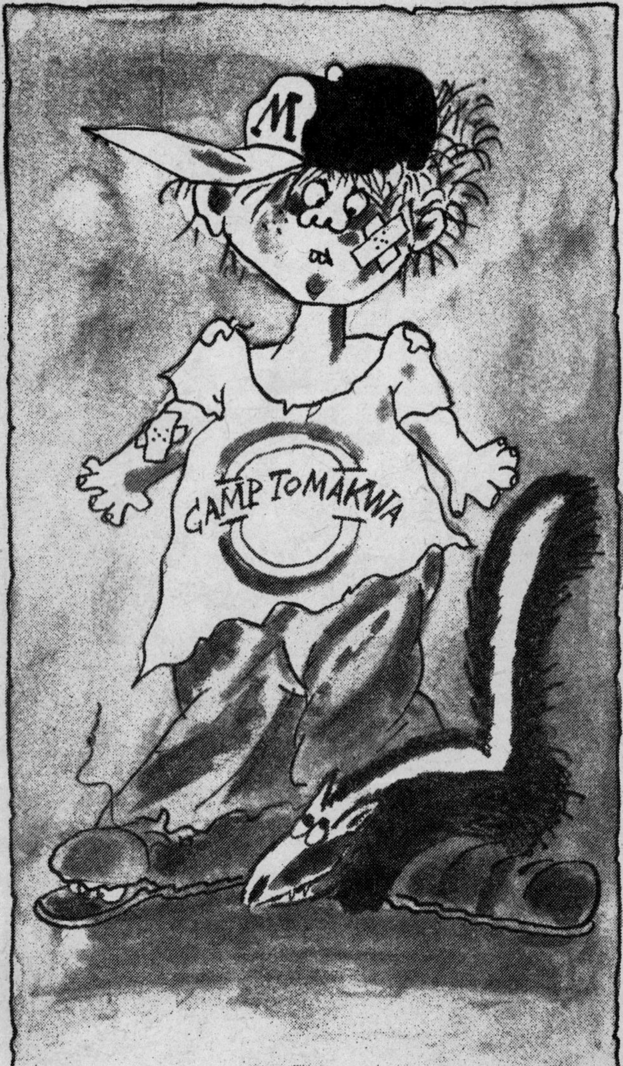
M
CAMP TOMAKWA

First time away from home

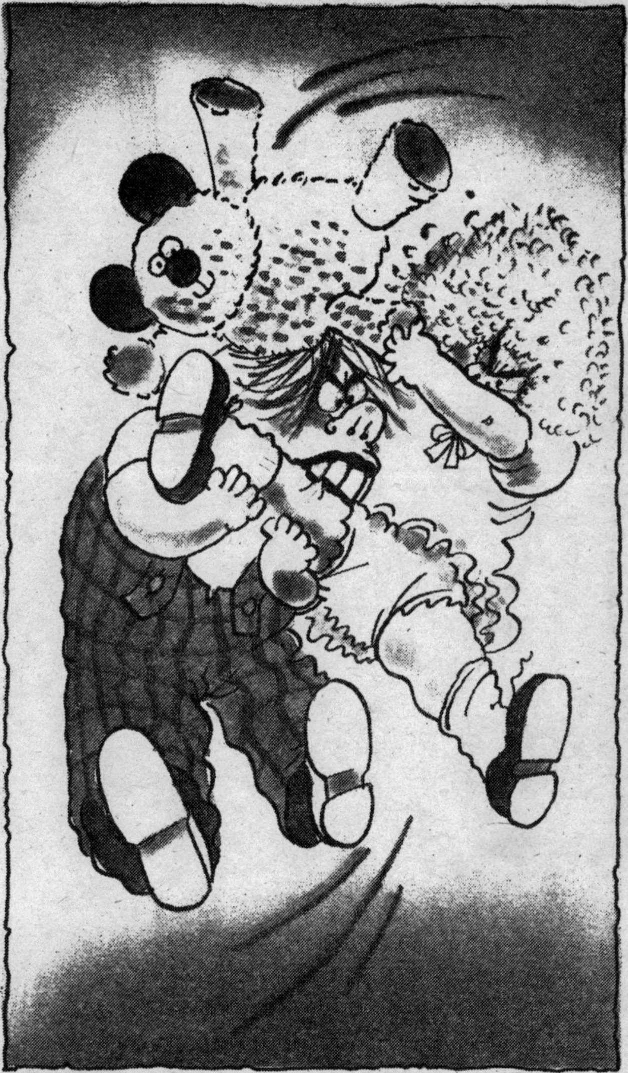

First time alone with a member of the opposite sex

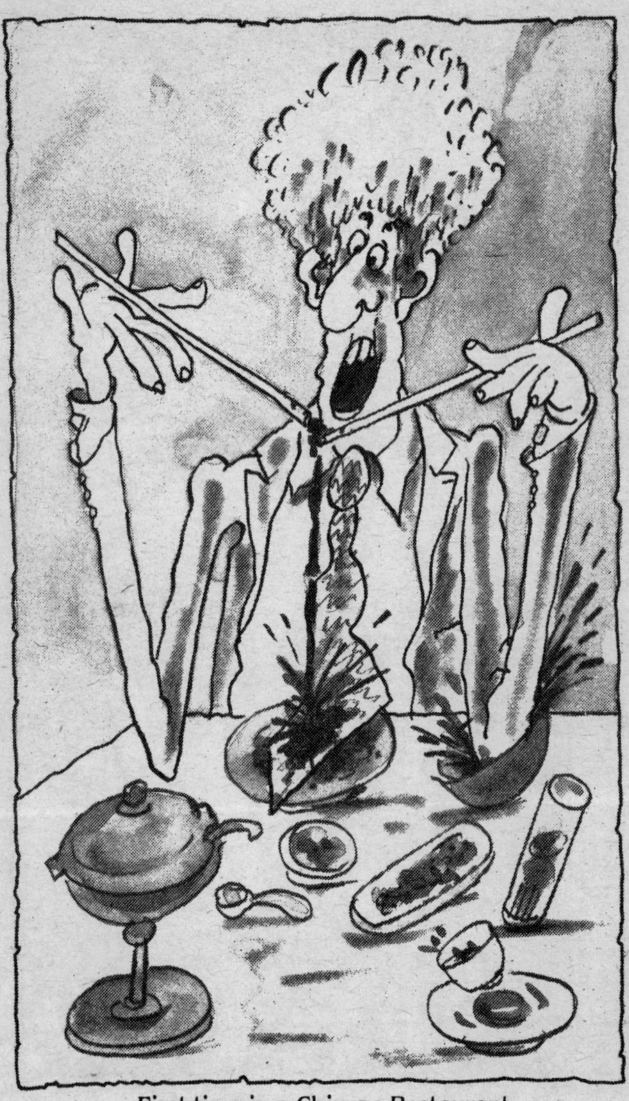

First time in a Chinese Restaurant

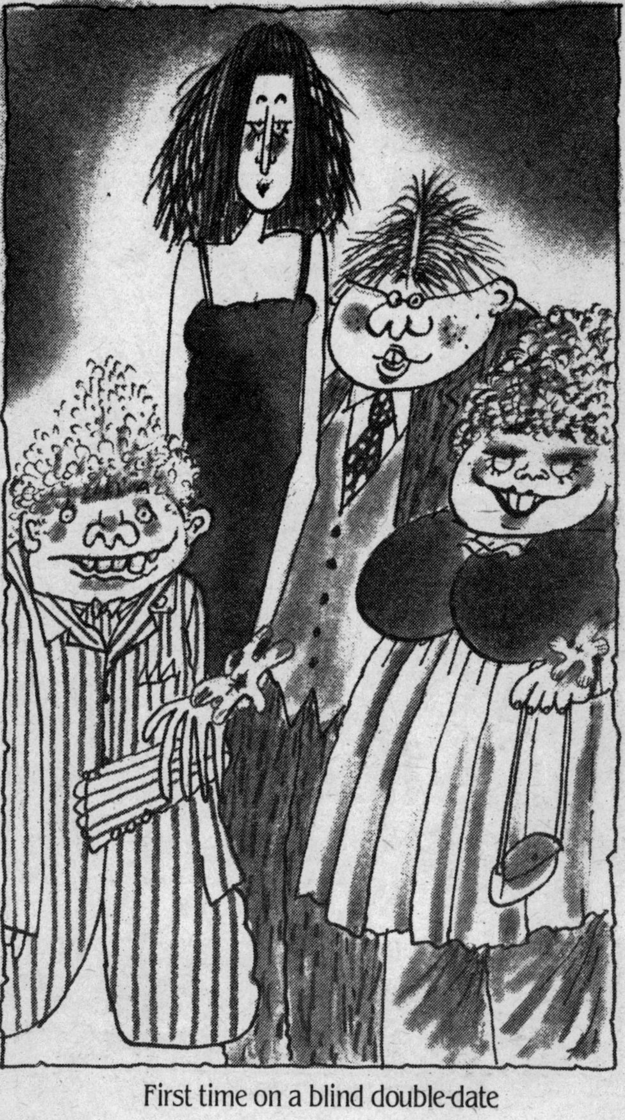

First time on a blind double-date

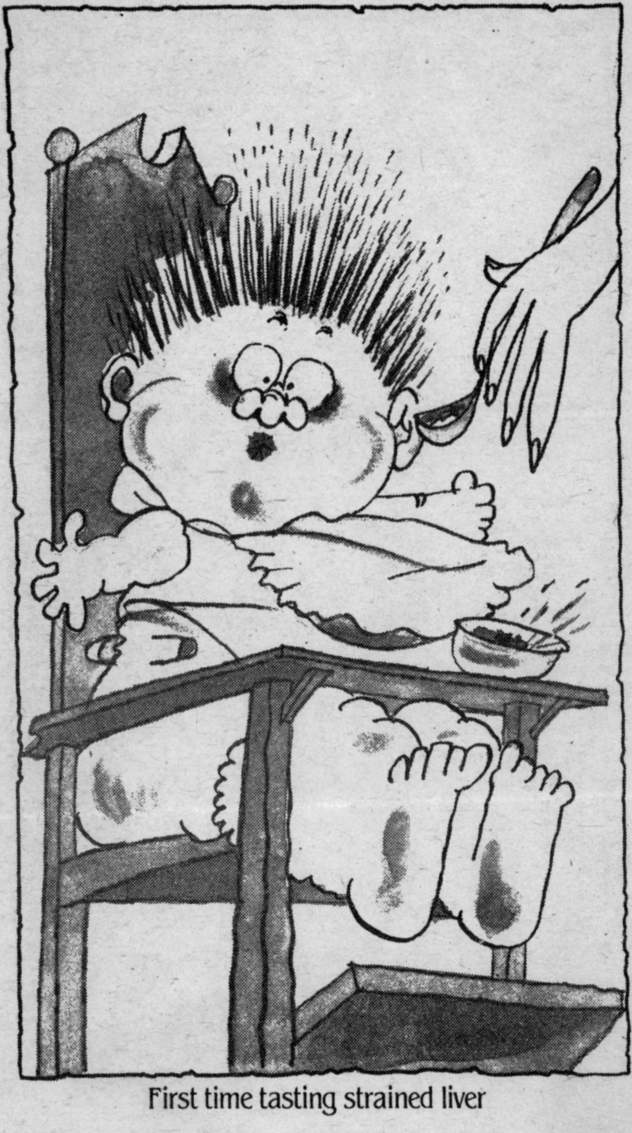

First time tasting strained liver

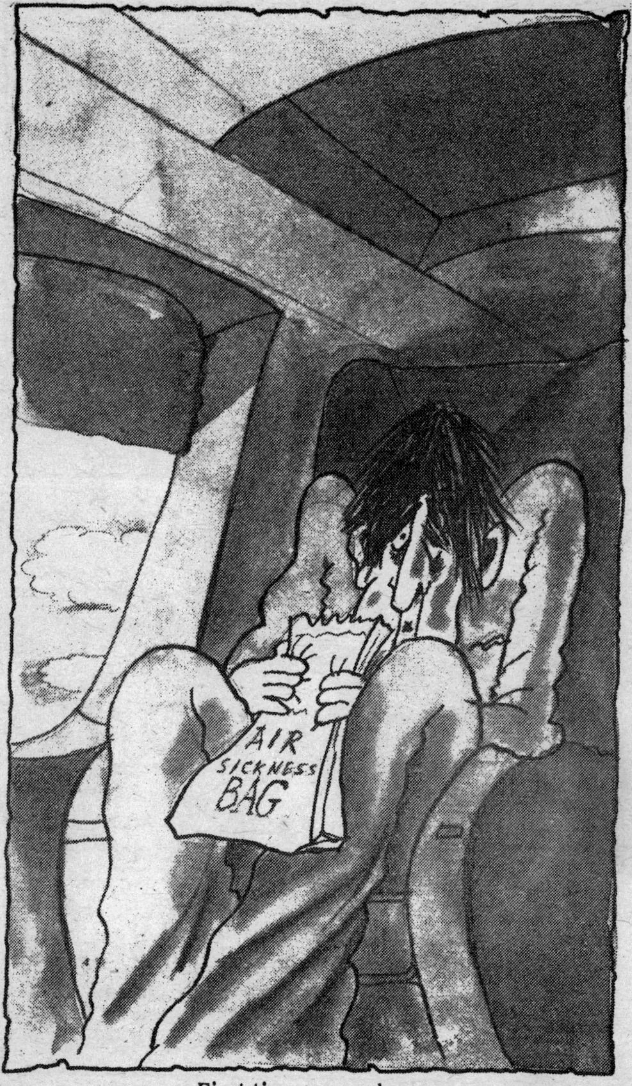
AIR
SICKNESS
BAG

First time on a plane

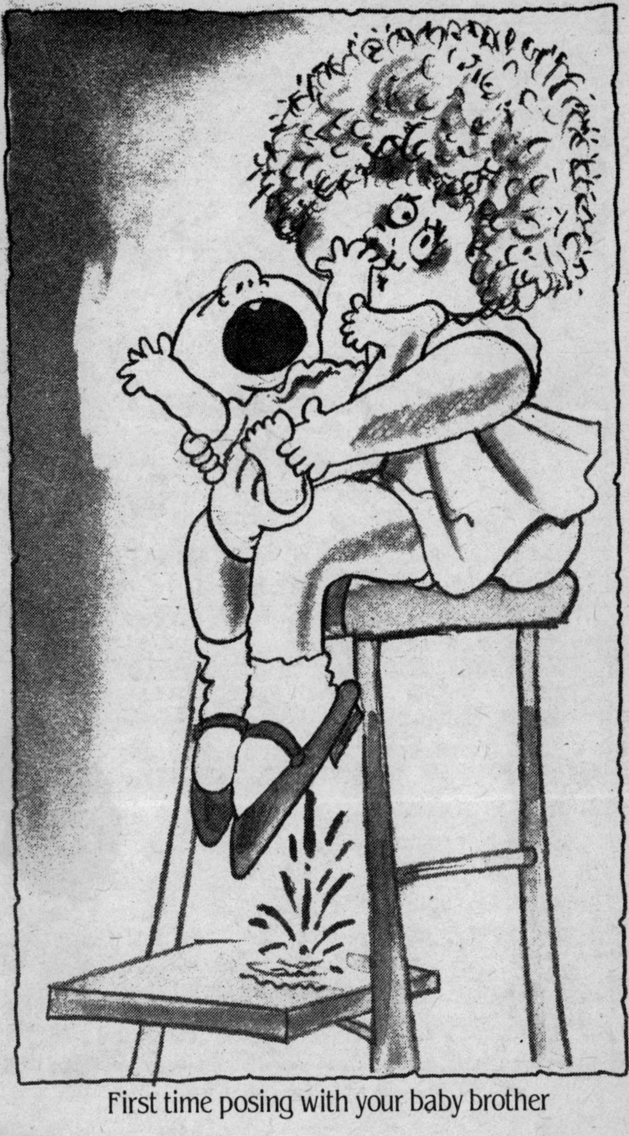

First time posing with your baby brother

NOT-SO-FAMOUS LAST WORDS IN PHOTOGRAPHY

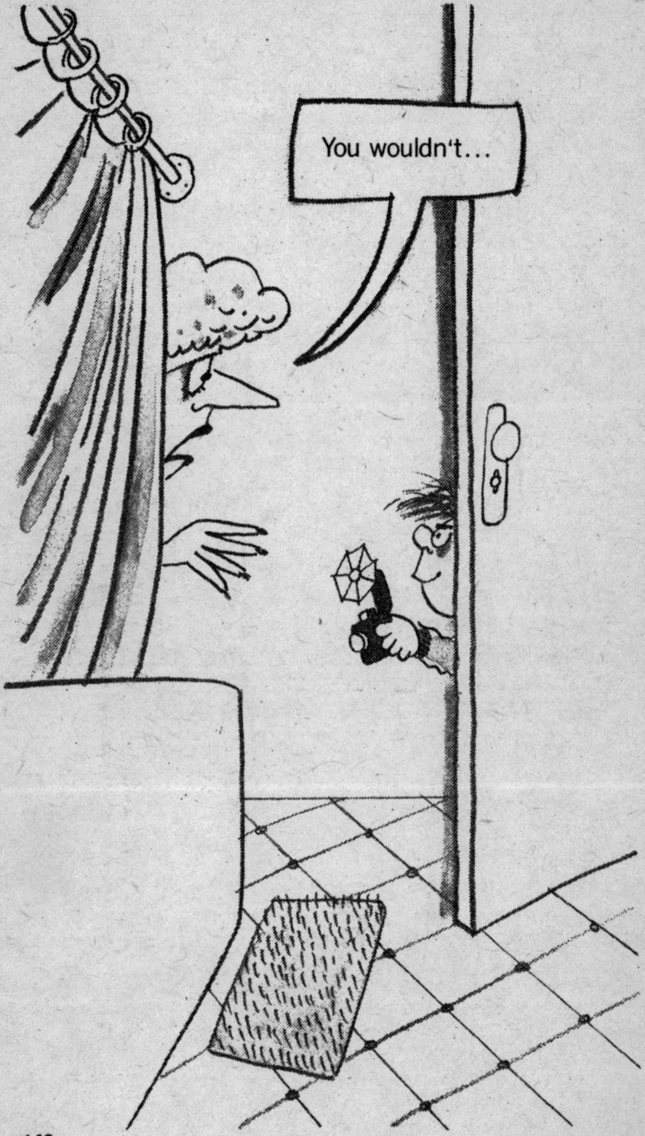
You wouldn't...

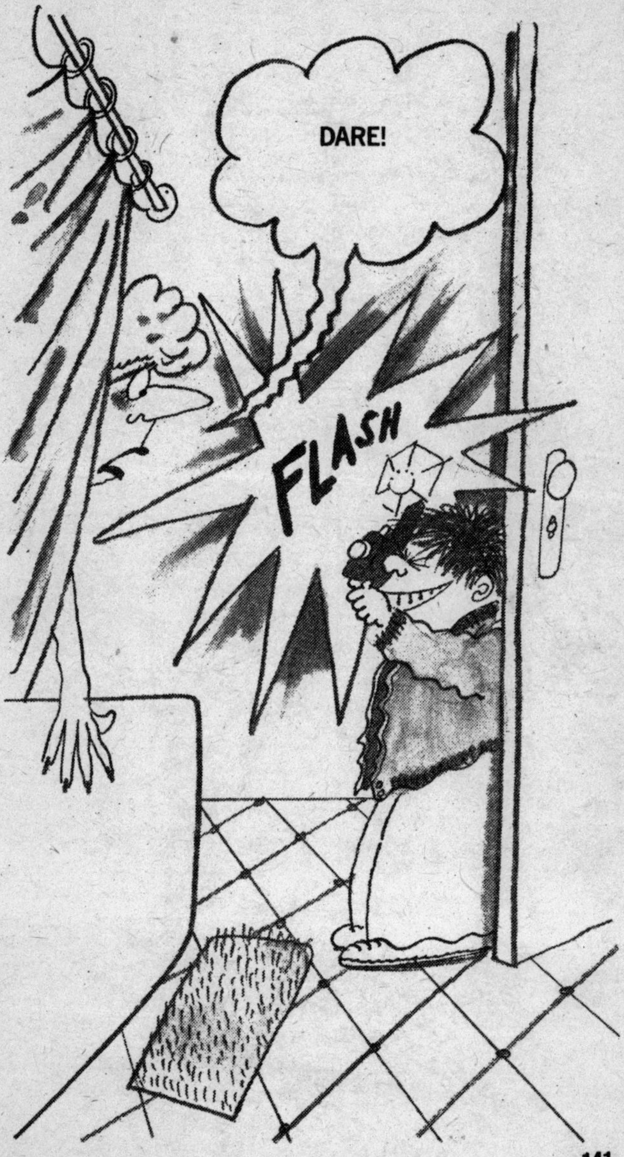
DARE!
FLASH

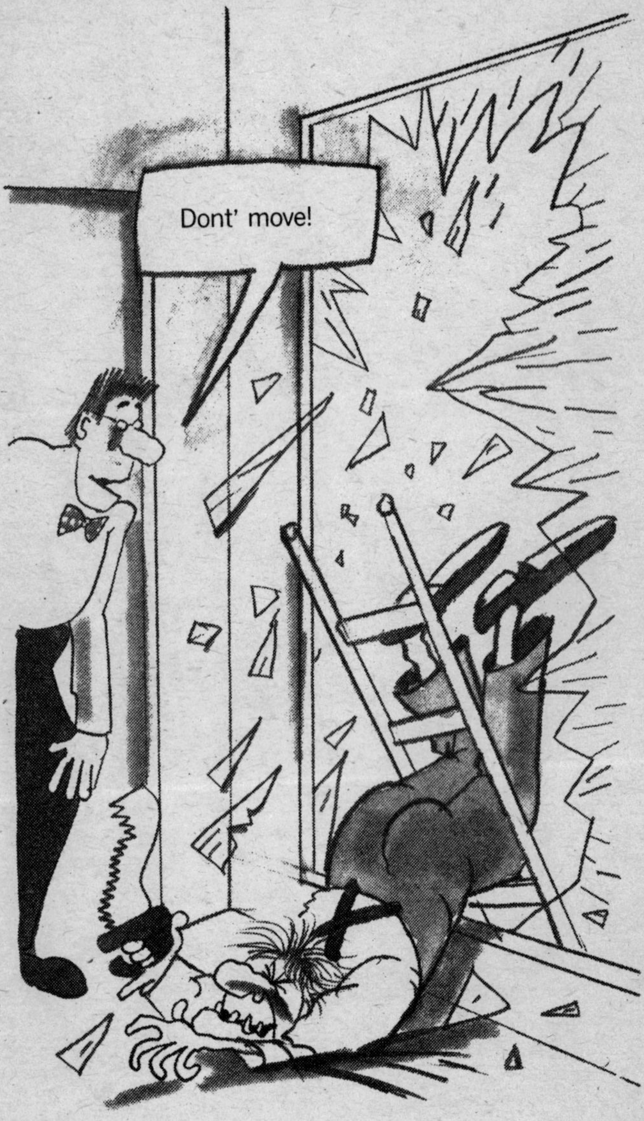
Dont' move!

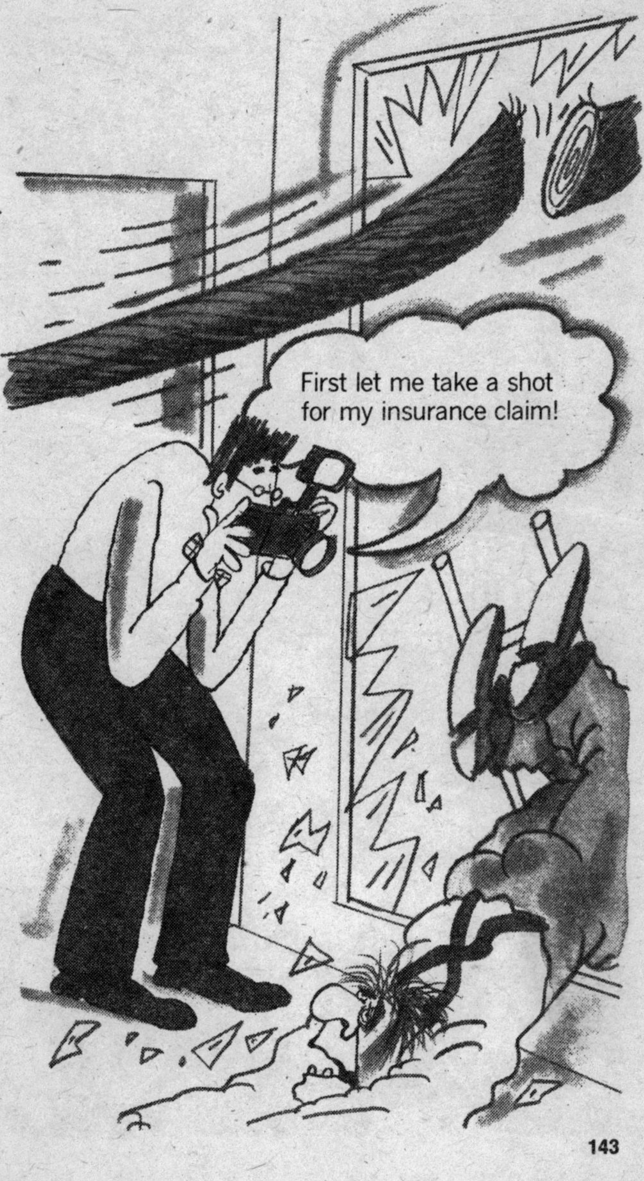
First let me take a shot for my insurance claim!

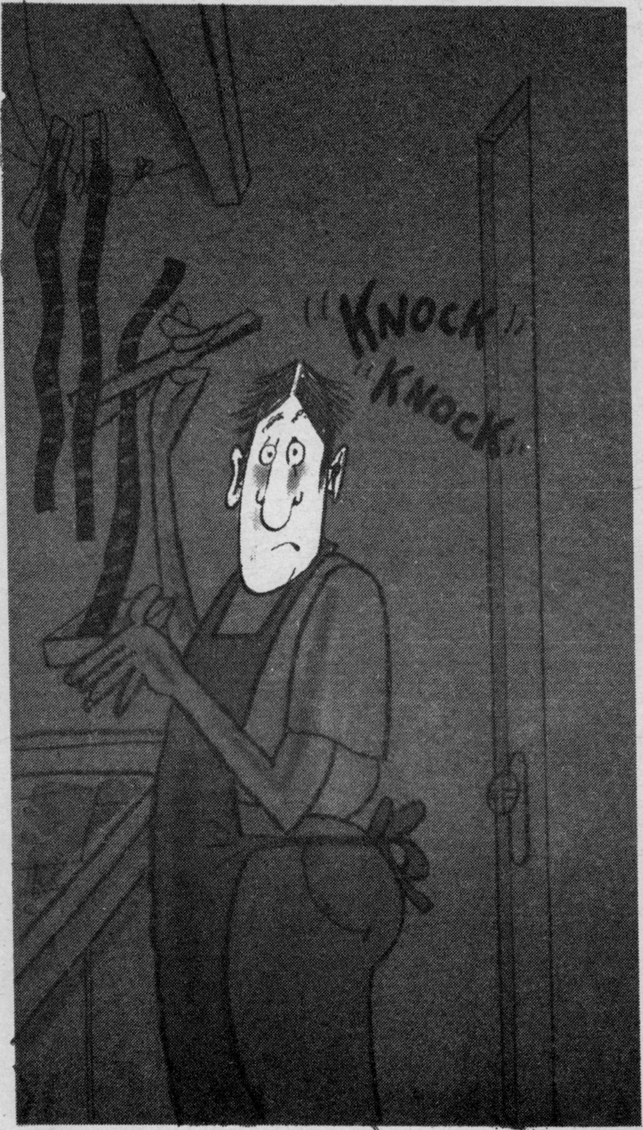
KNOCK
KNOCK

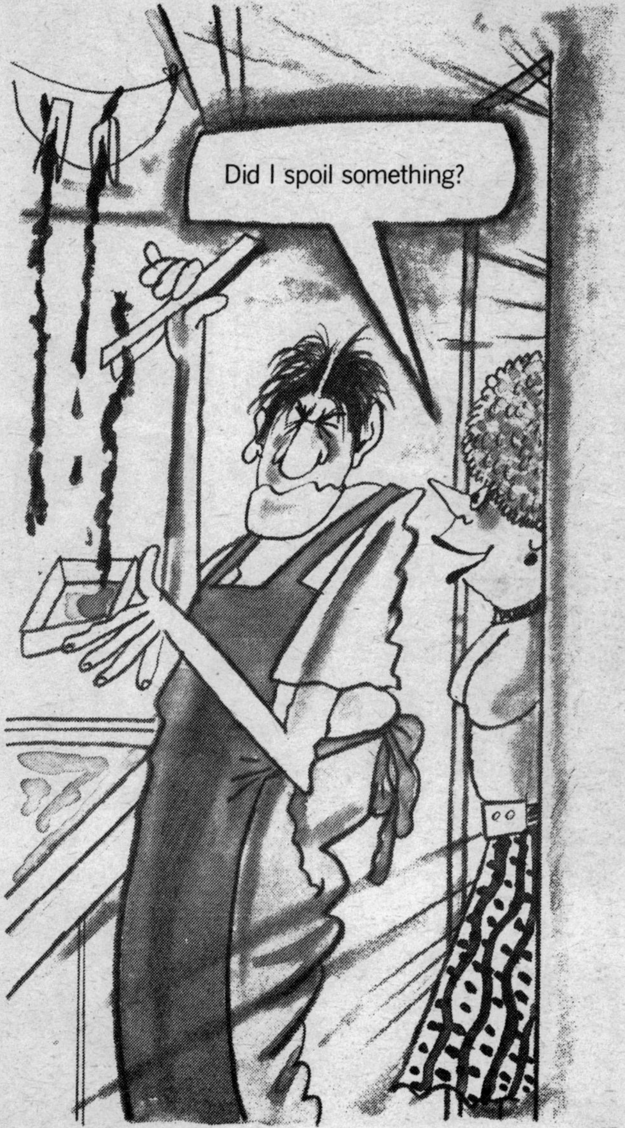
Did I spoil something?

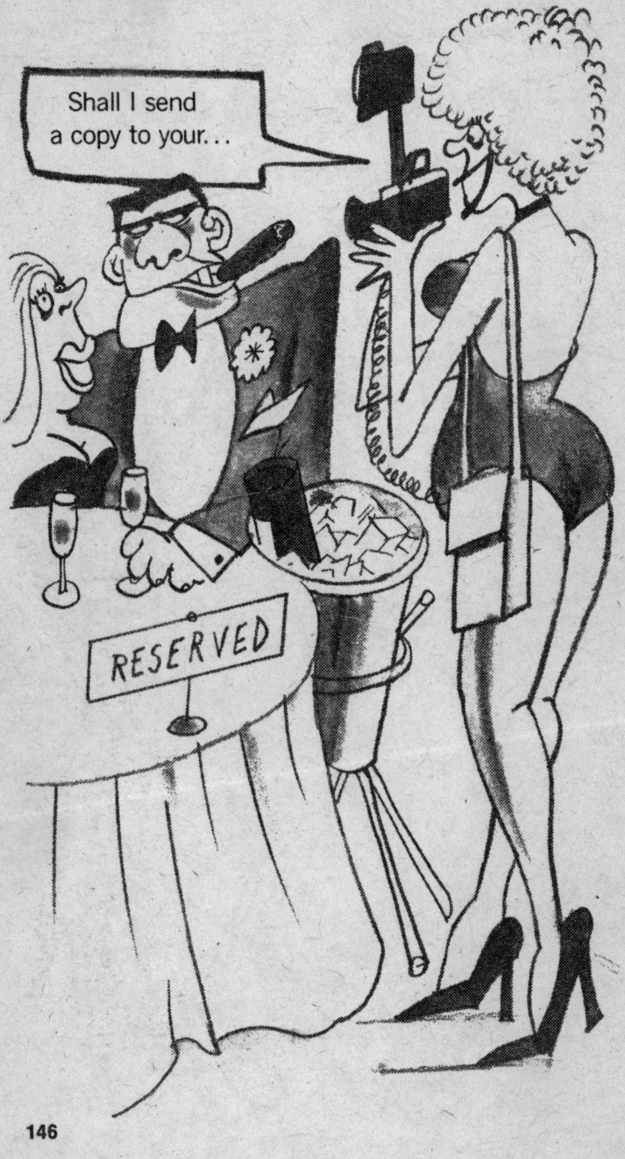
Shall I send
a copy to your. . .
RESERVED

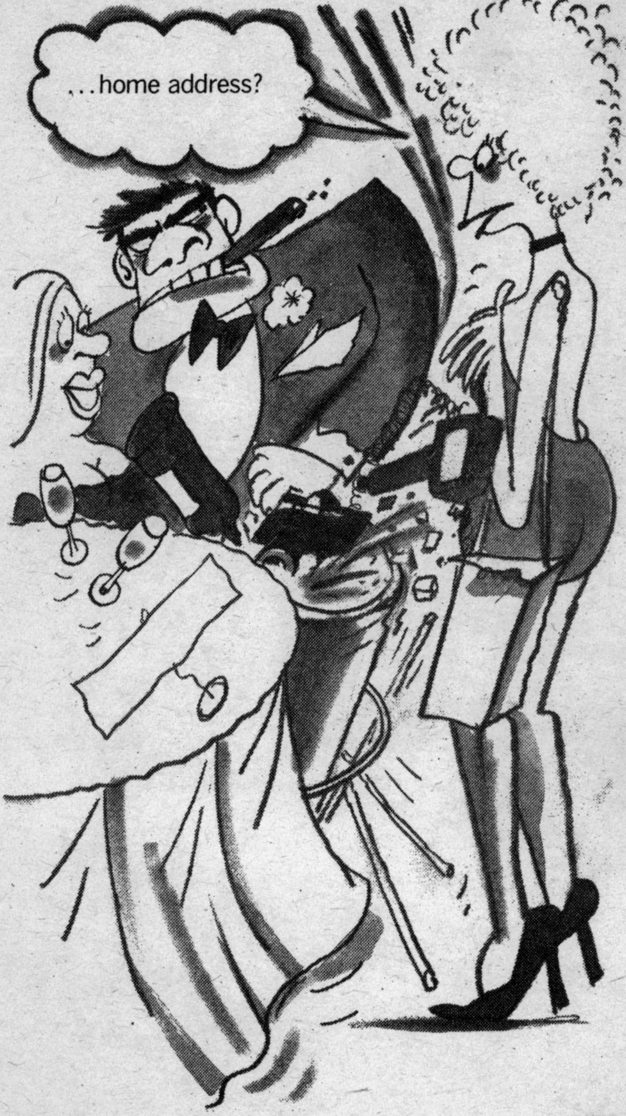
...home address?

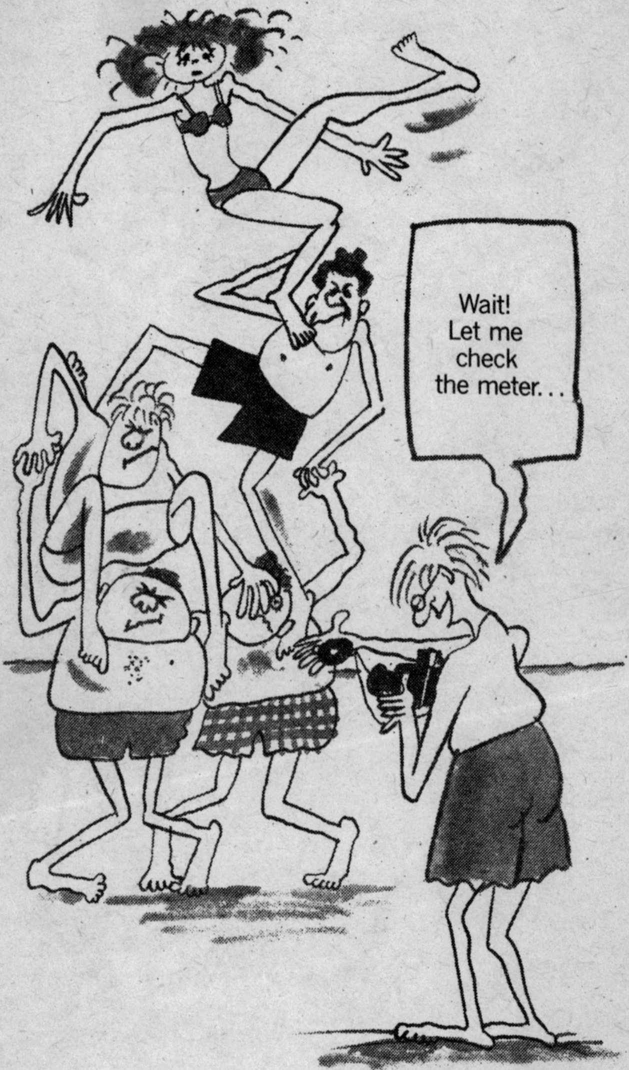
Wait!
Let me
check
the meter...

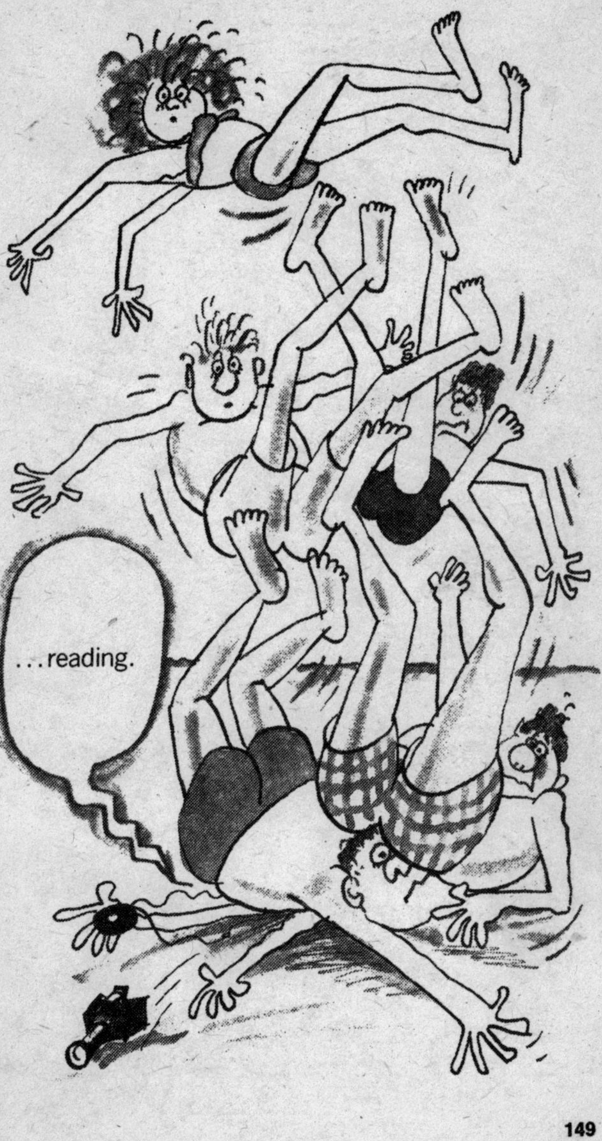
...reading.

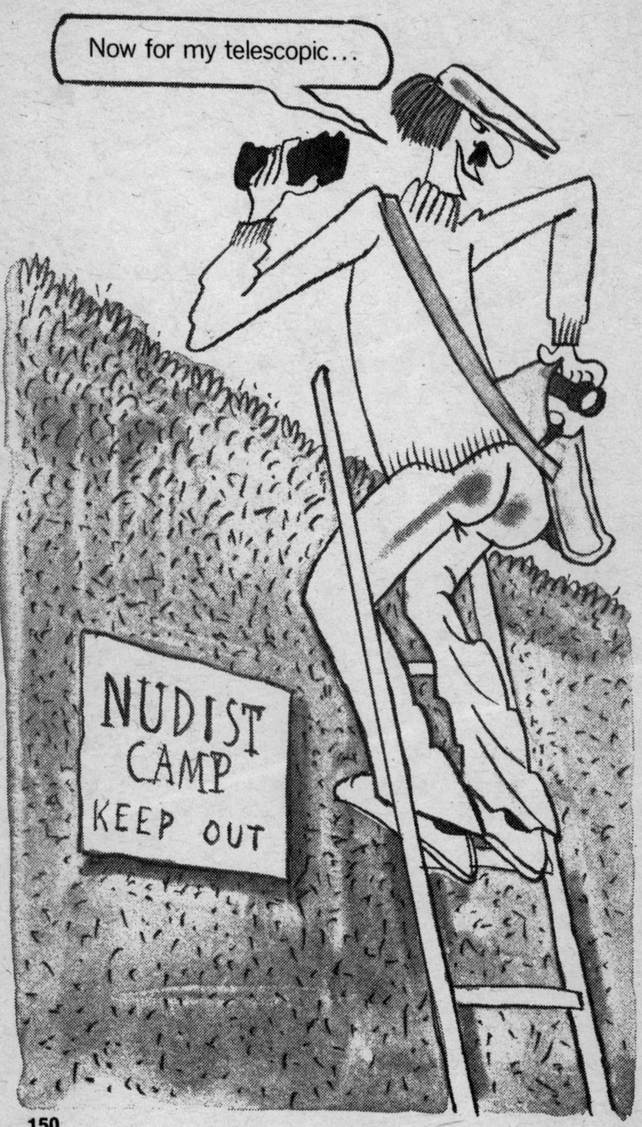
Now for my telescopic...
NUDIST
CAMP
KEEP OUT

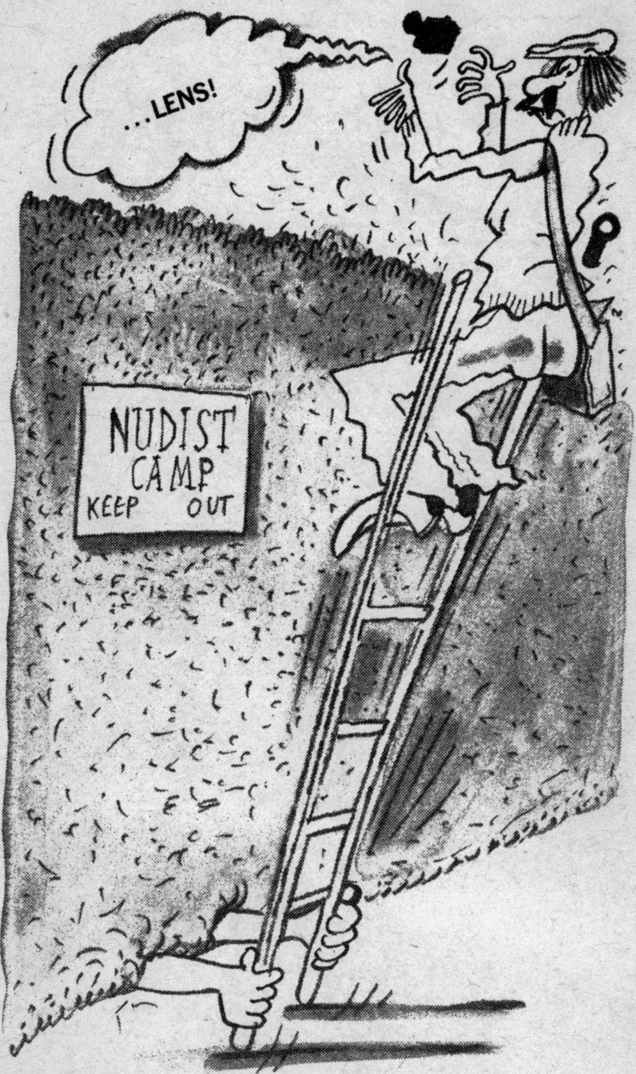
...LENS!
NUDIST CAMP
KEEP OUT

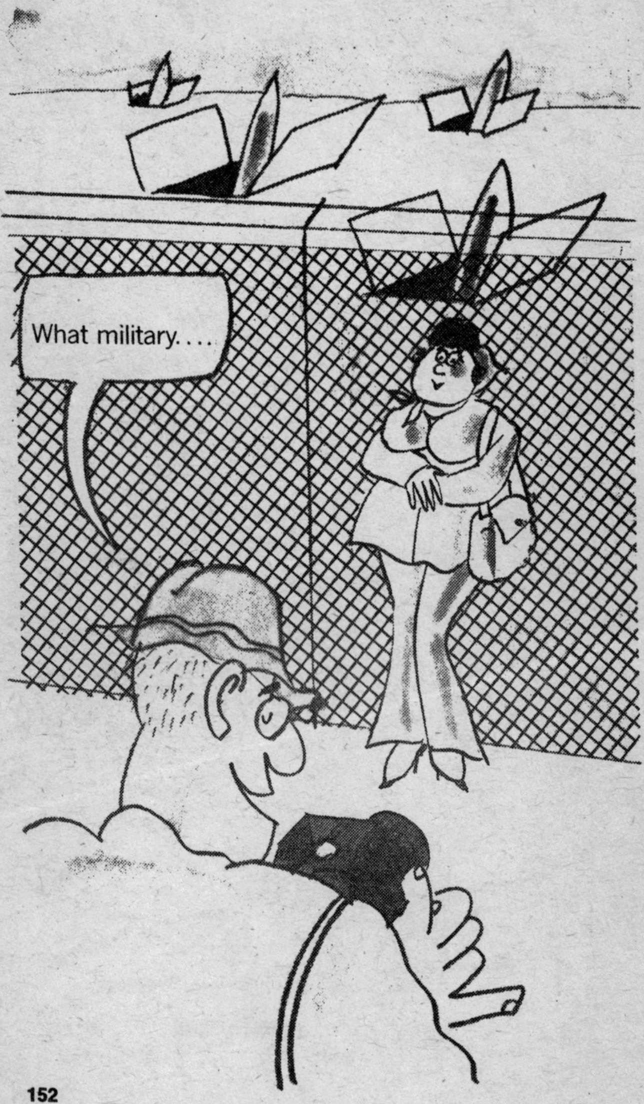
What military. . . .

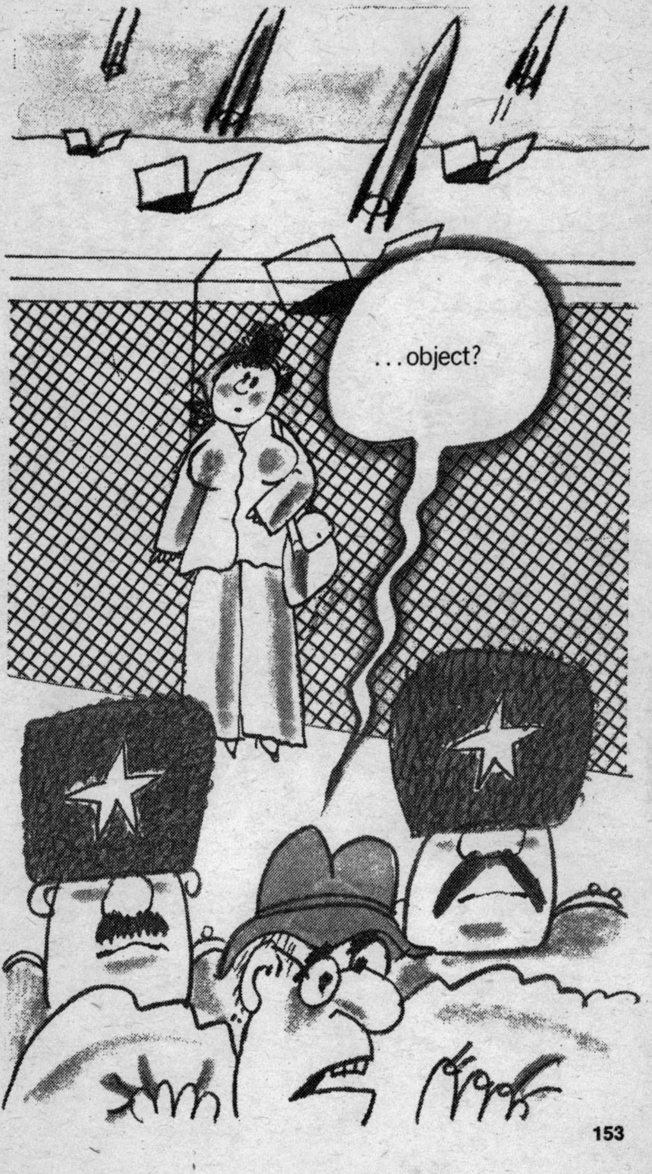
...object?

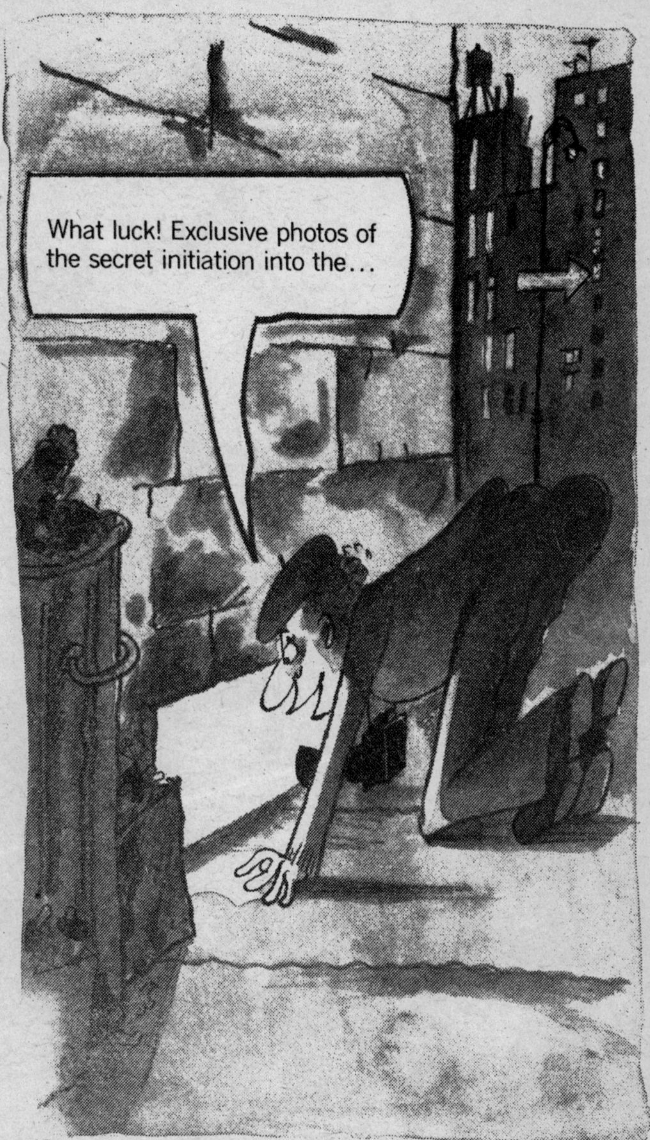
What luck! Exclusive photos of the secret initiation into the...

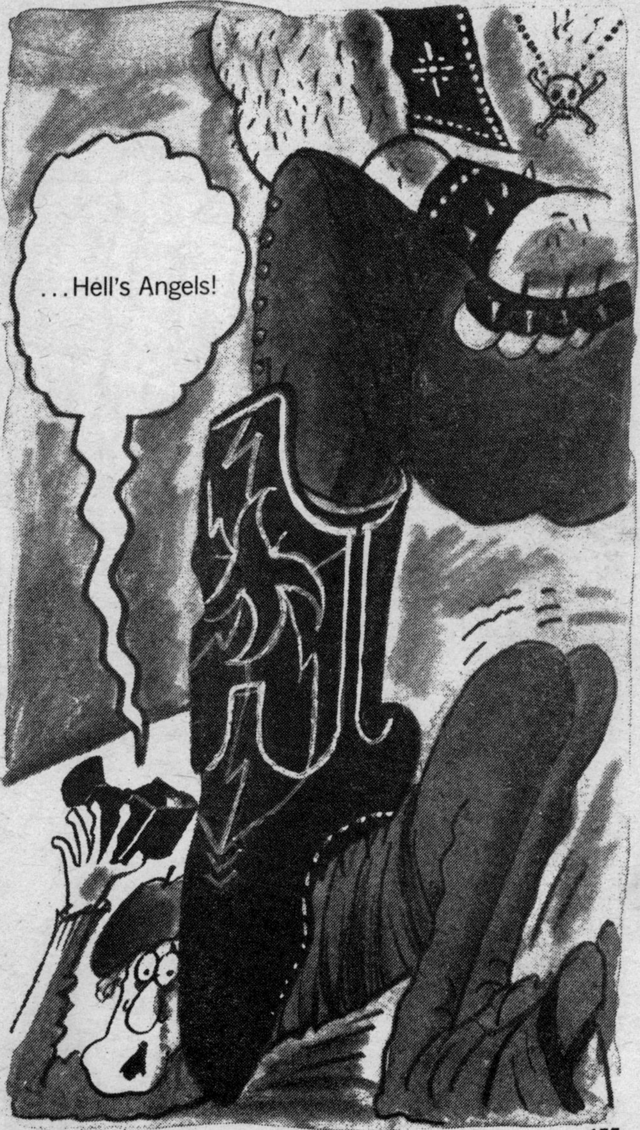
...Hell's Angels!

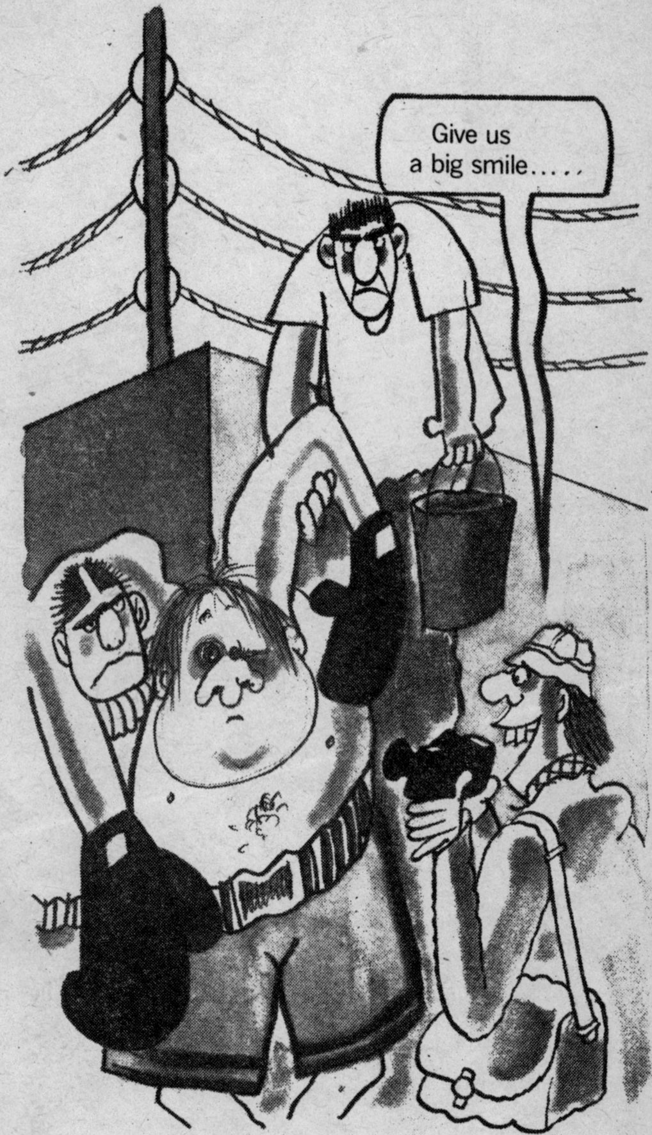
Give us
a big smile.....

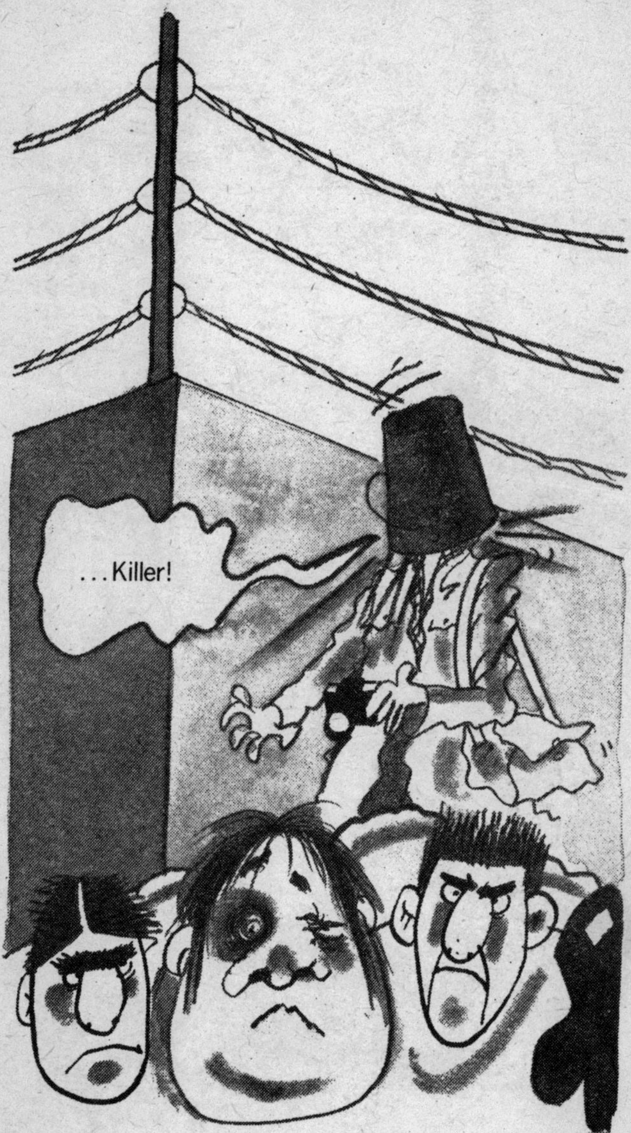
. . . Killer!

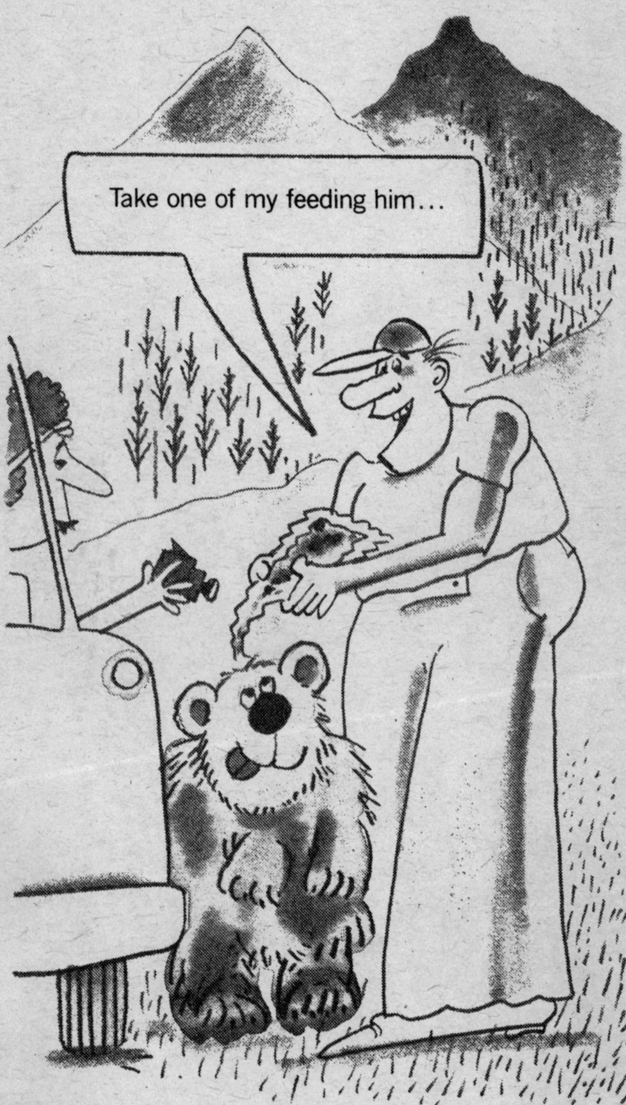
Take one of my feeding him...

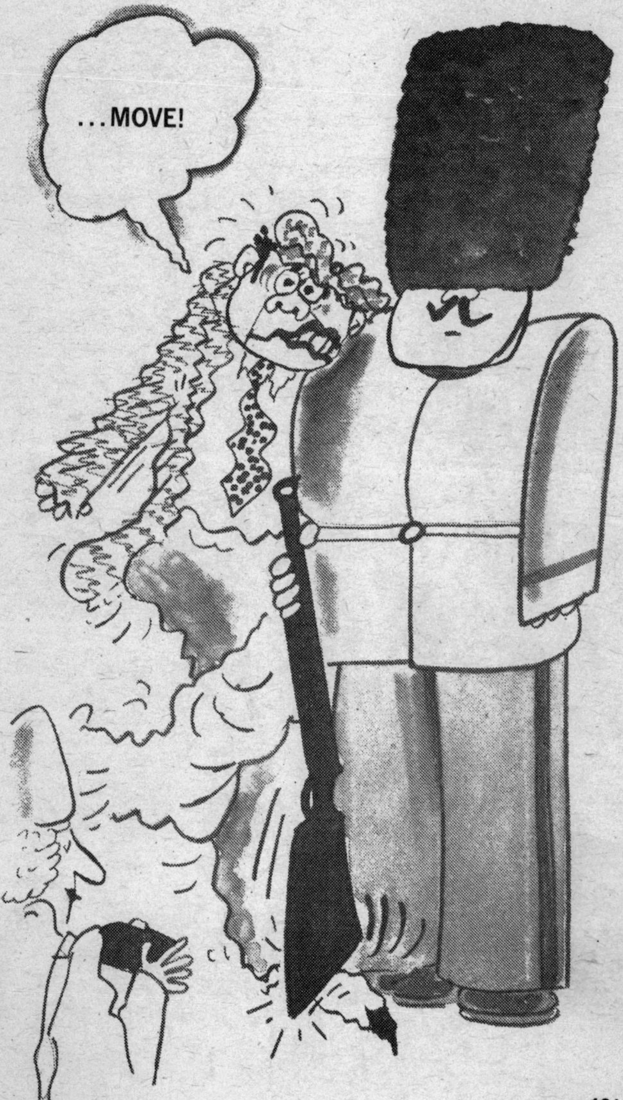
...MOVE!

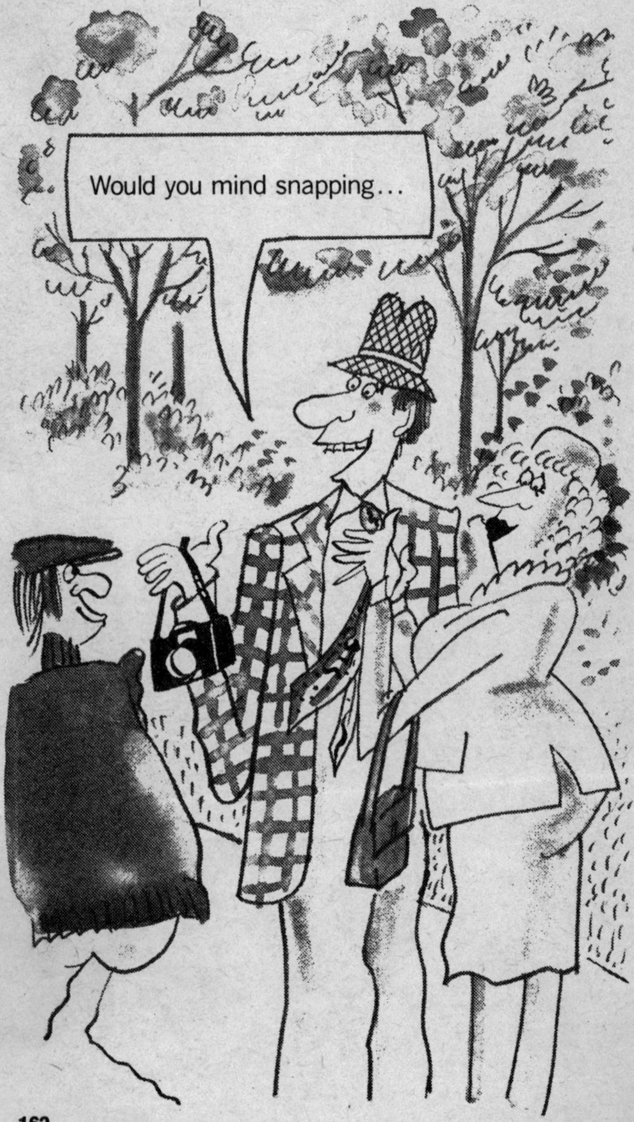
Would you mind snapping…

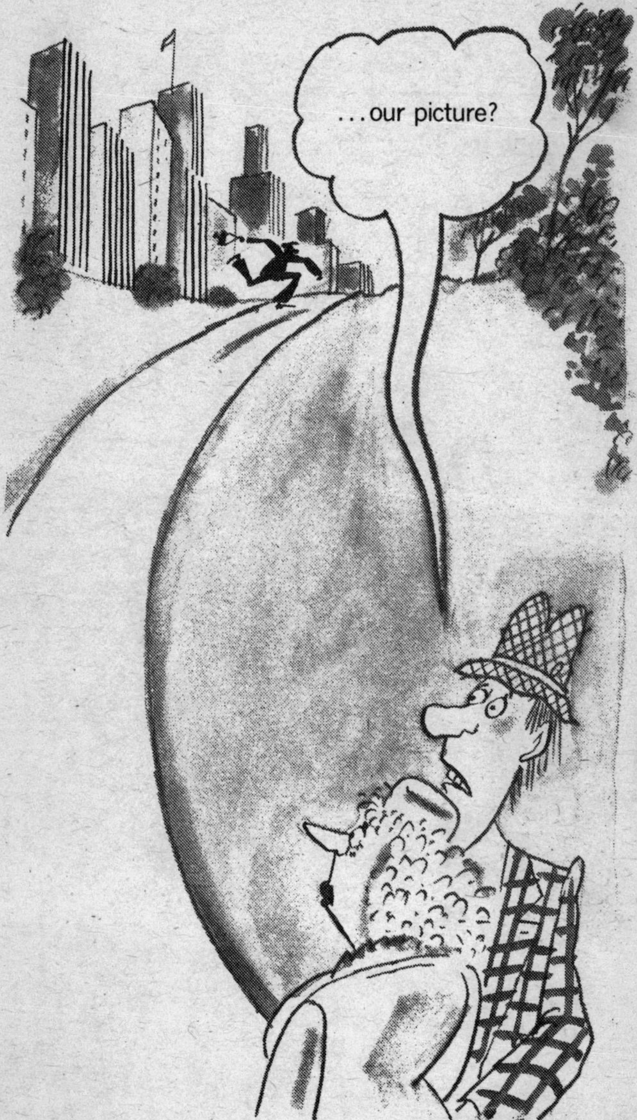
...our picture?

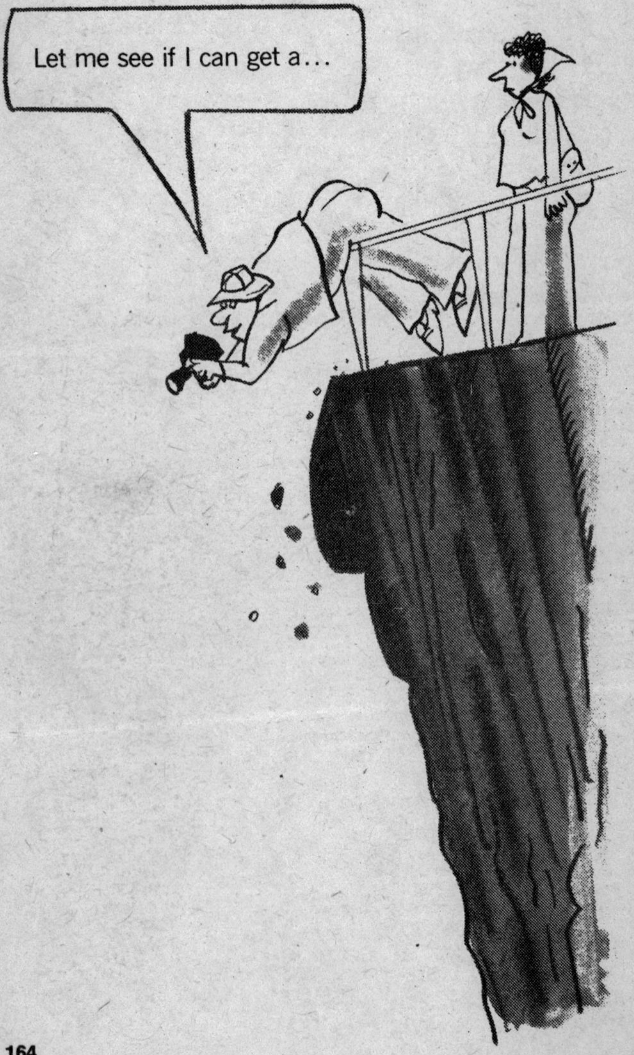
Let me see if I can get a...

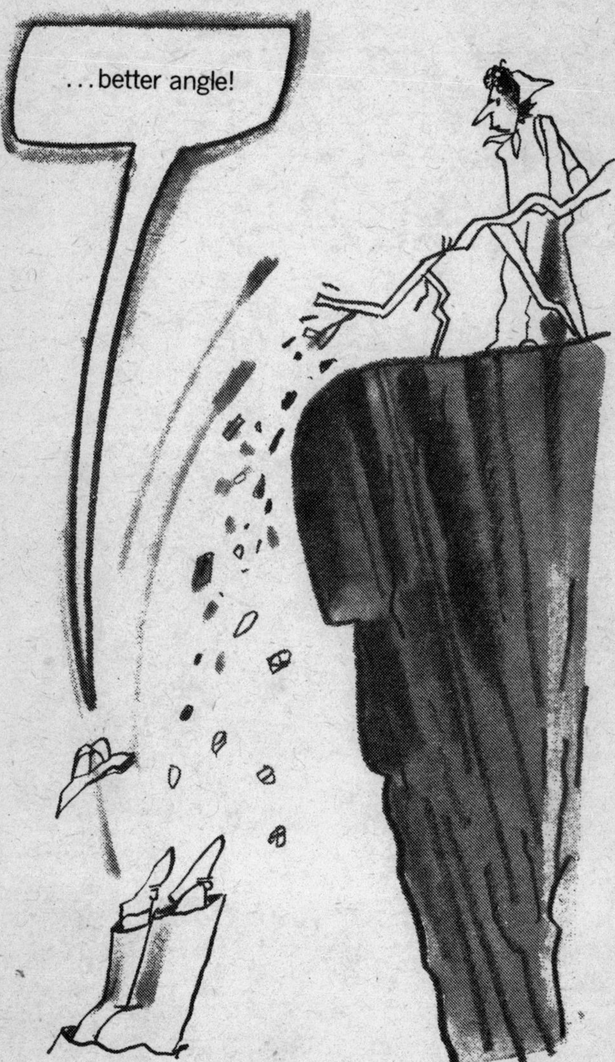
. . . better angle!

ON A WILDLIFE PHOTO SAFARI

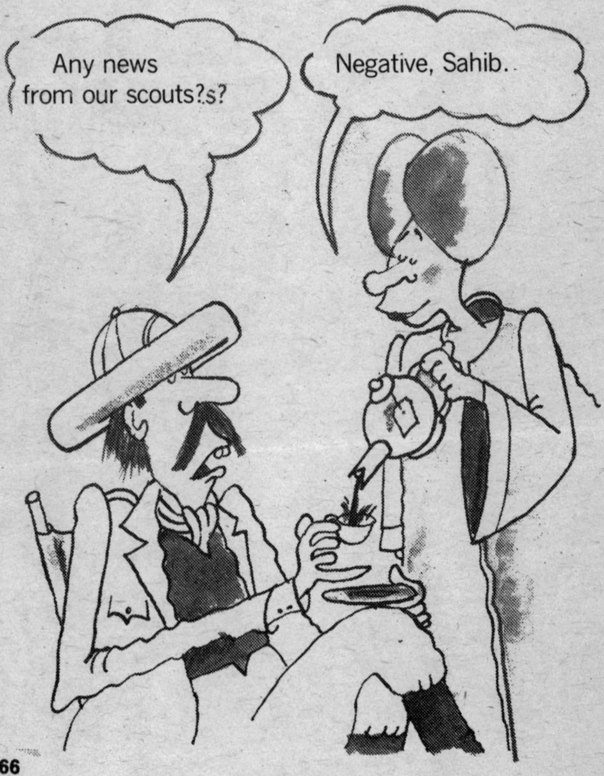
Any news from our scouts?.s?
Negative, Sahib..

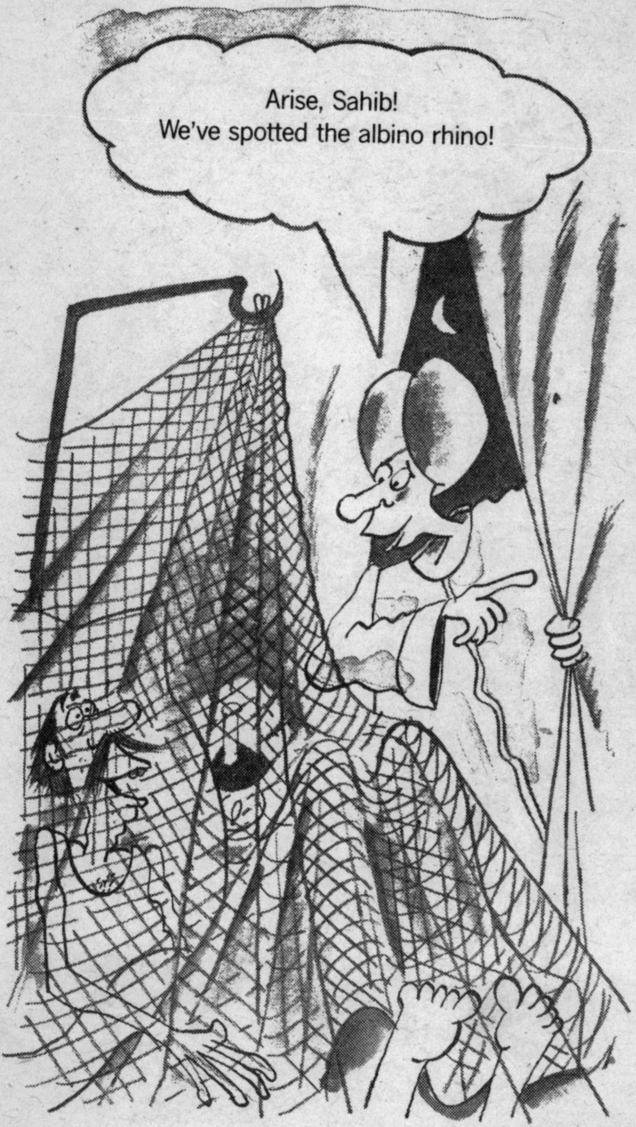
Arise, Sahib!
We've spotted the albino rhino!

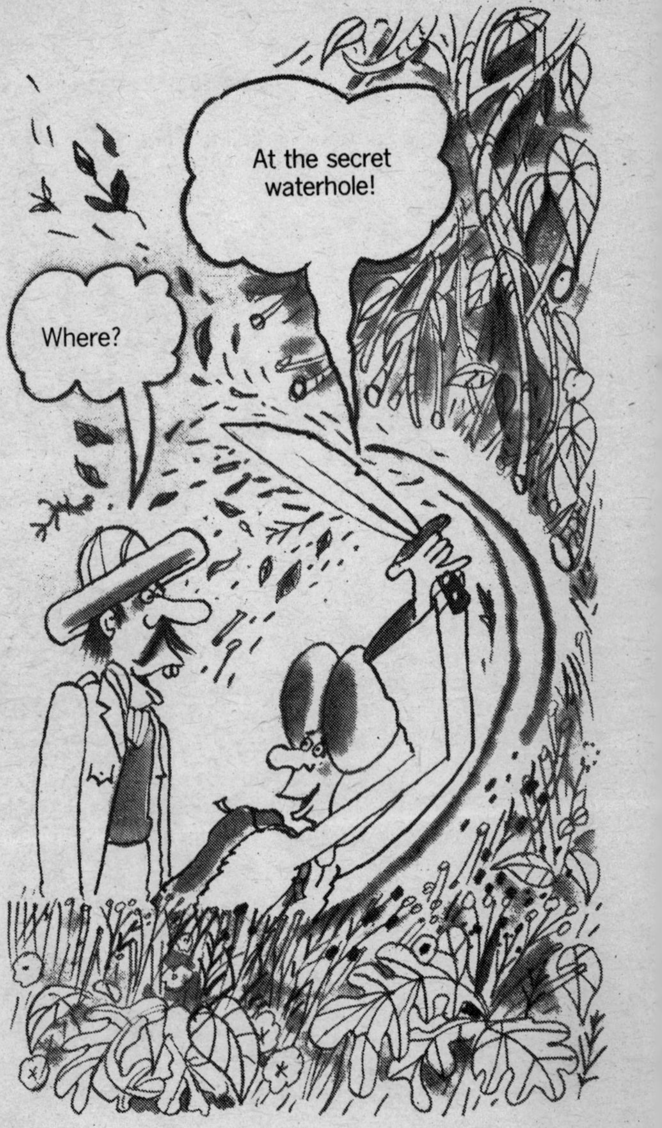
Where?
At the secret waterhole!

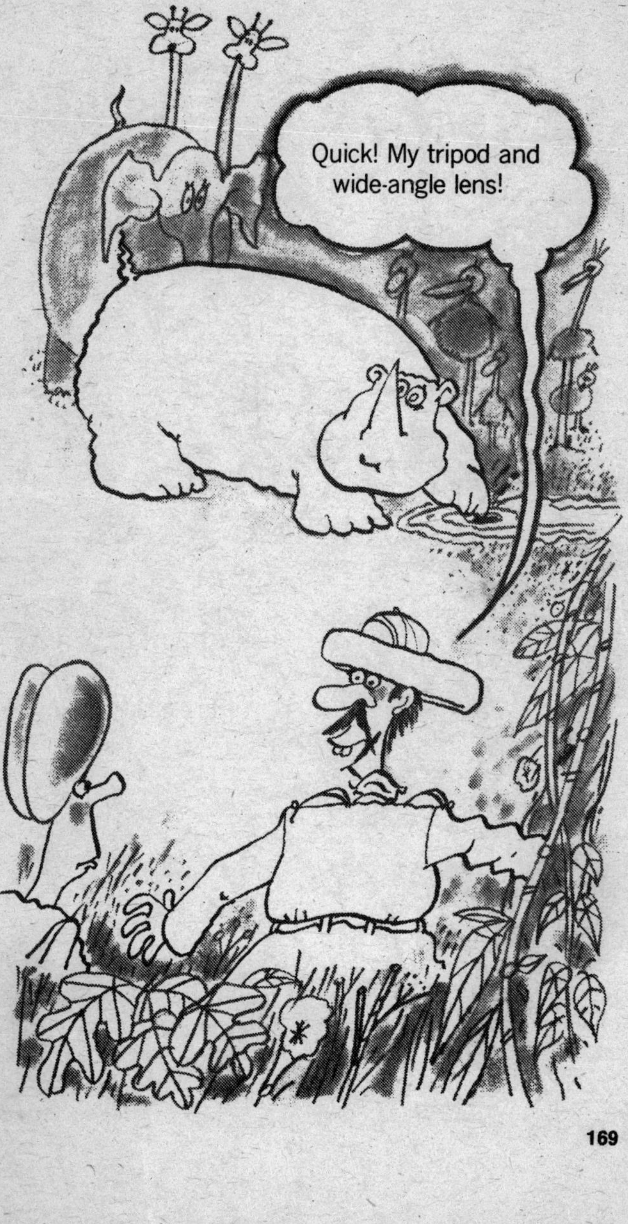
Quick! My tripod and wide-angle lens!

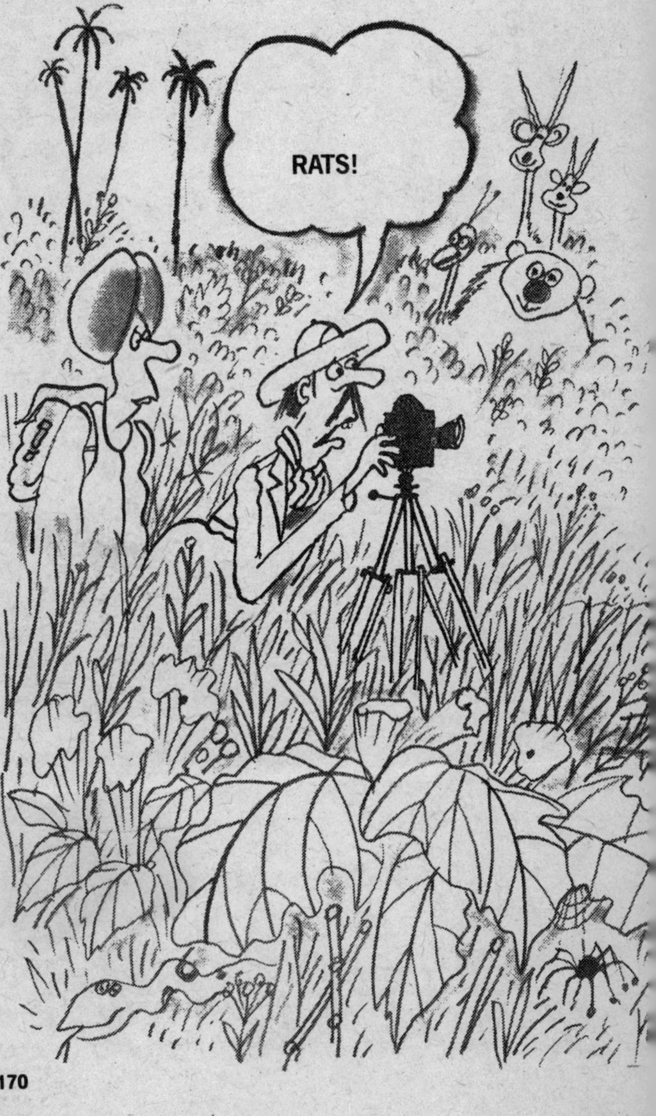
RATS!

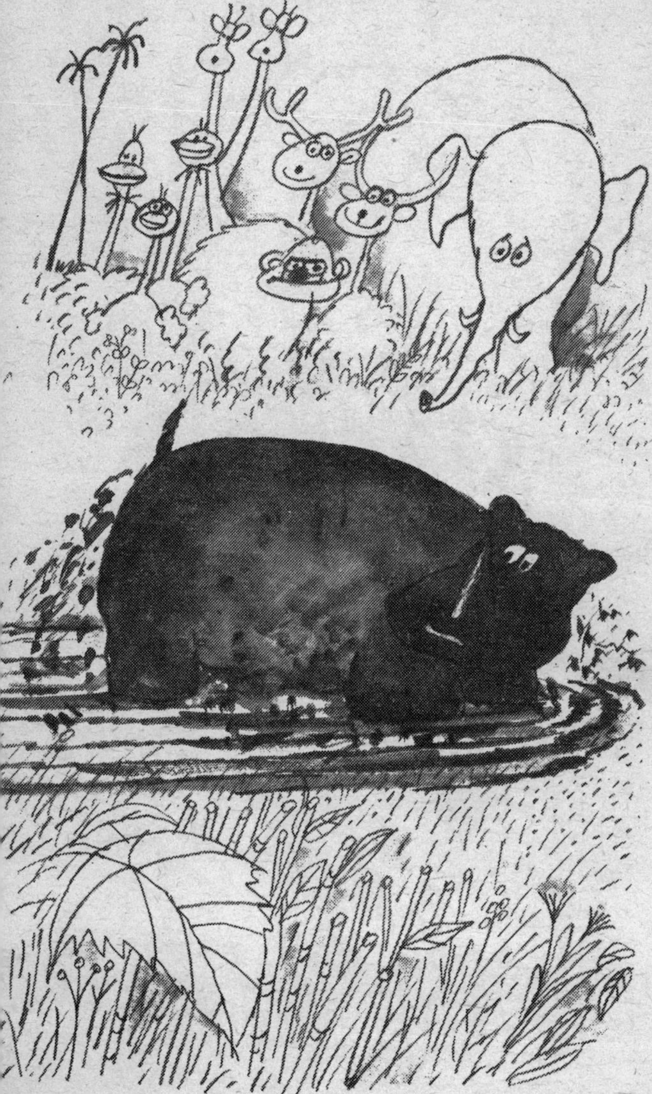

FAMOUS
BABY
PICTURES

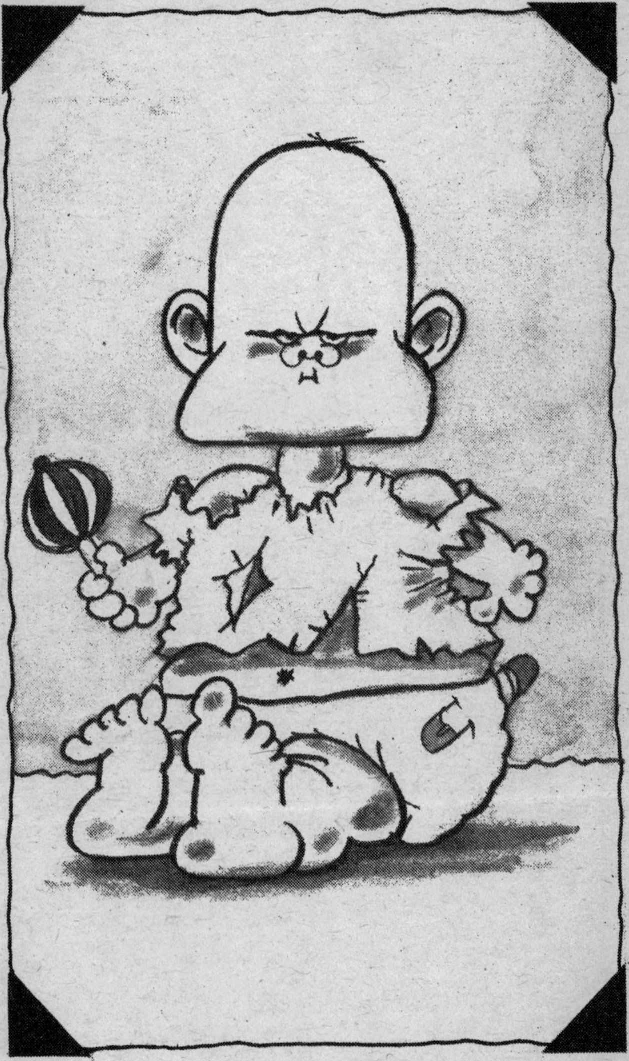

Marlon Brando in his first undershirt

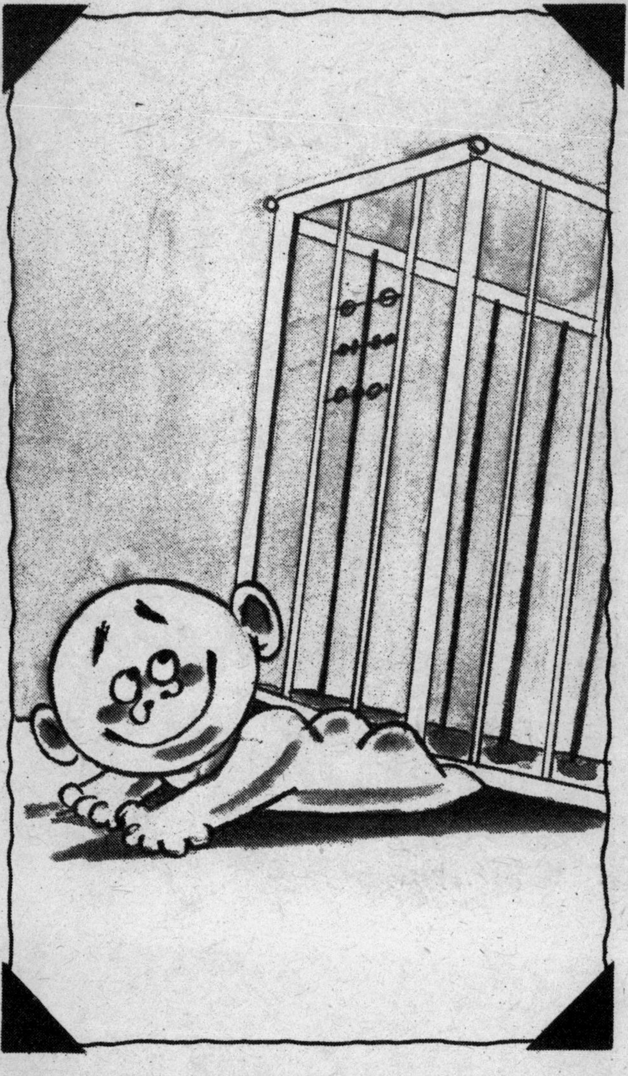

Houdini's first escape

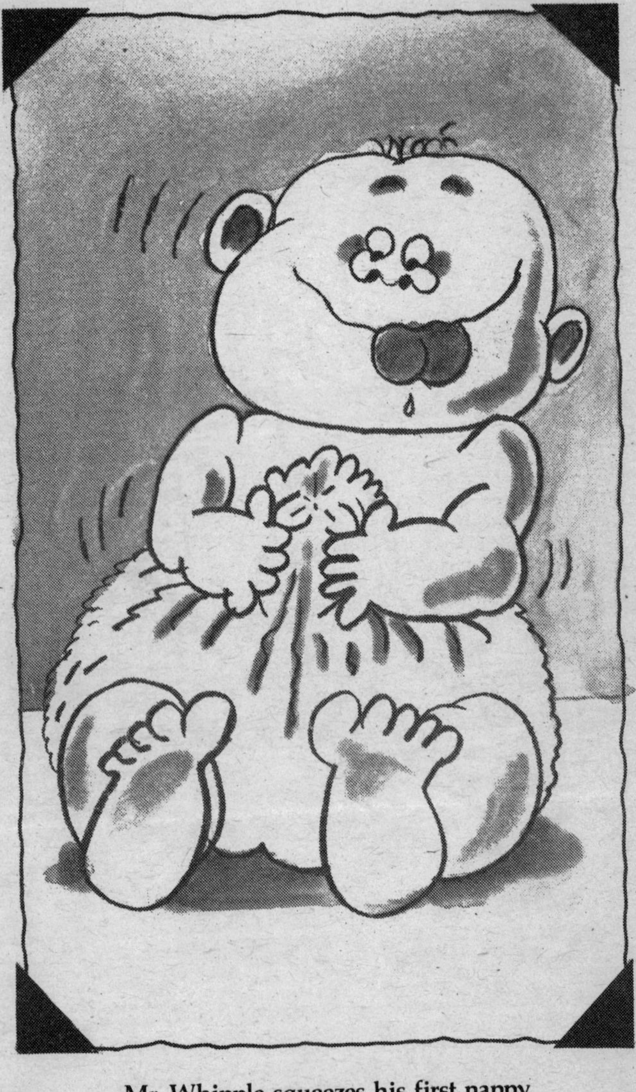

Mr. Whipple squeezes his first nappy

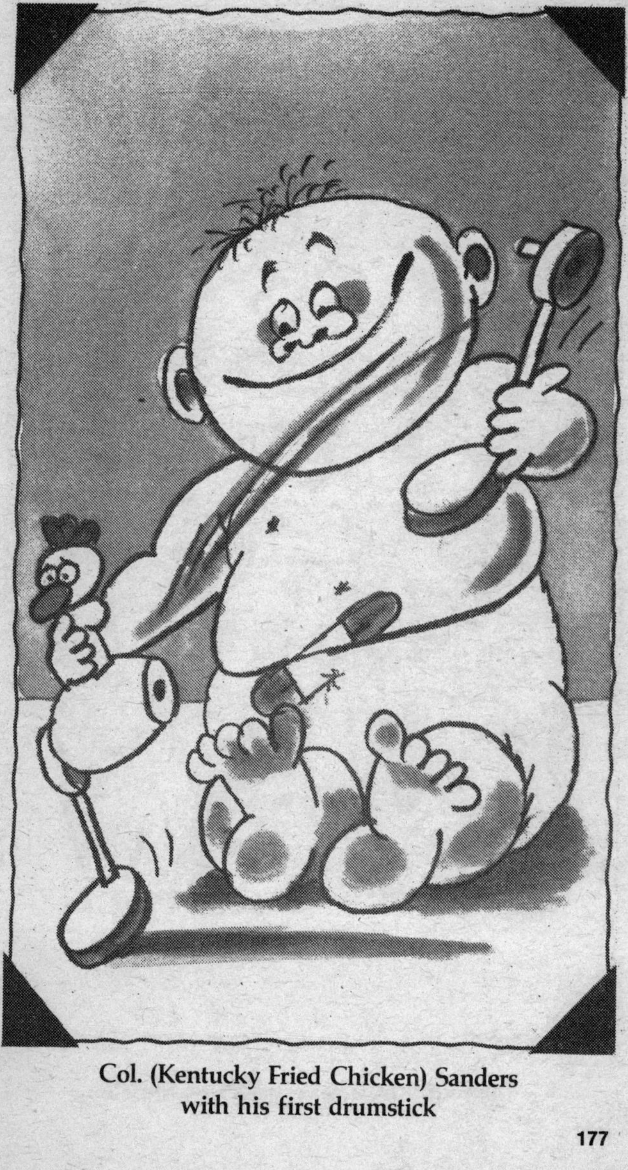

Col. (Kentucky Fried Chicken) Sanders
with his first drumstick

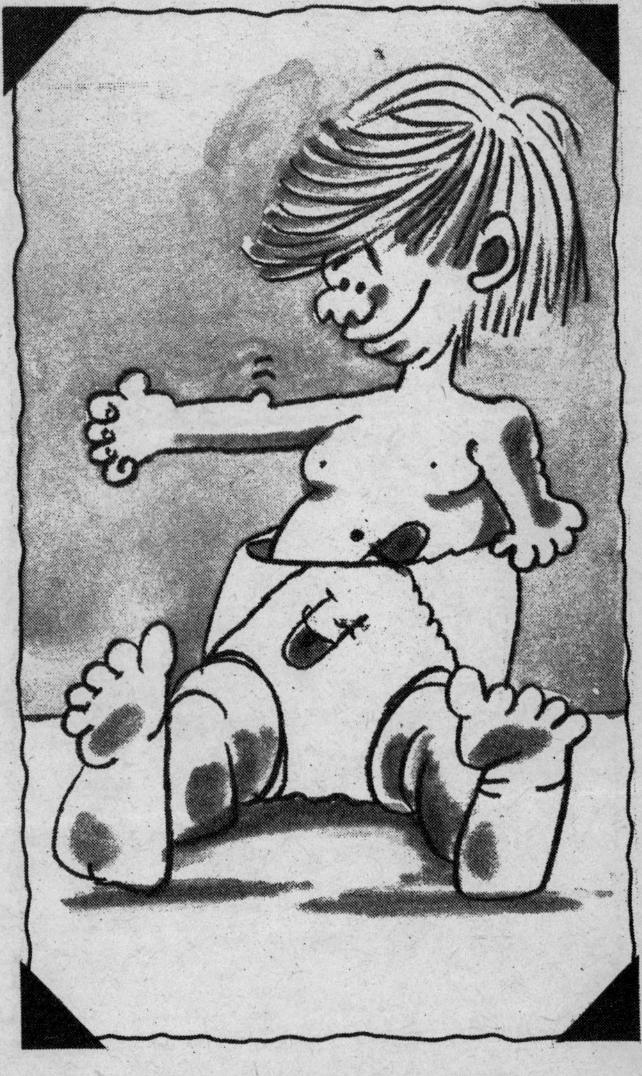

Arnold Schwarzenegger's first muscle

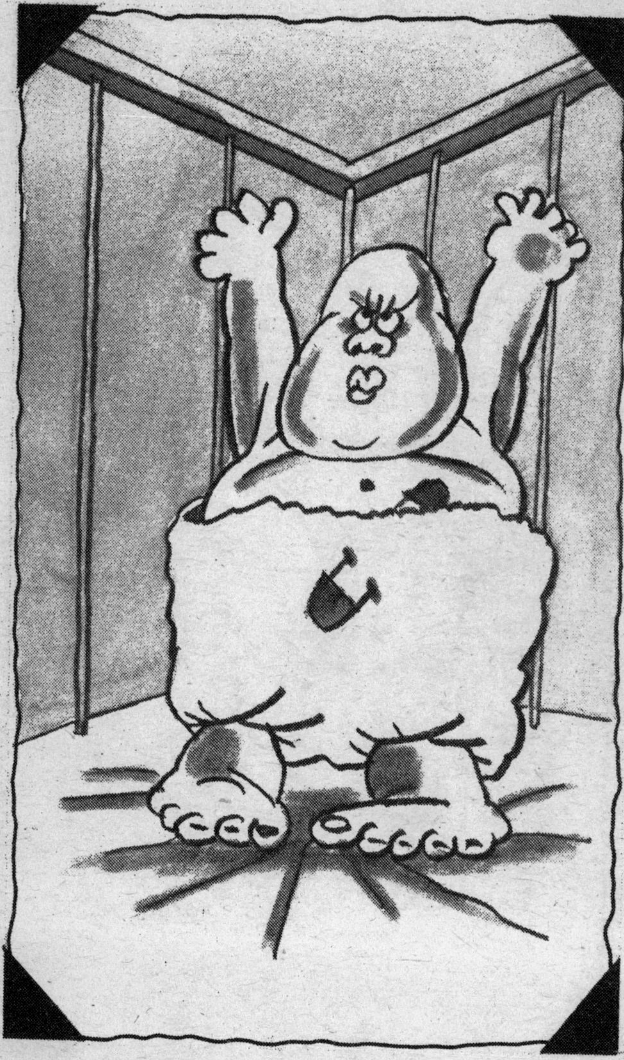

Sylvester Stallone in his first neutral corner

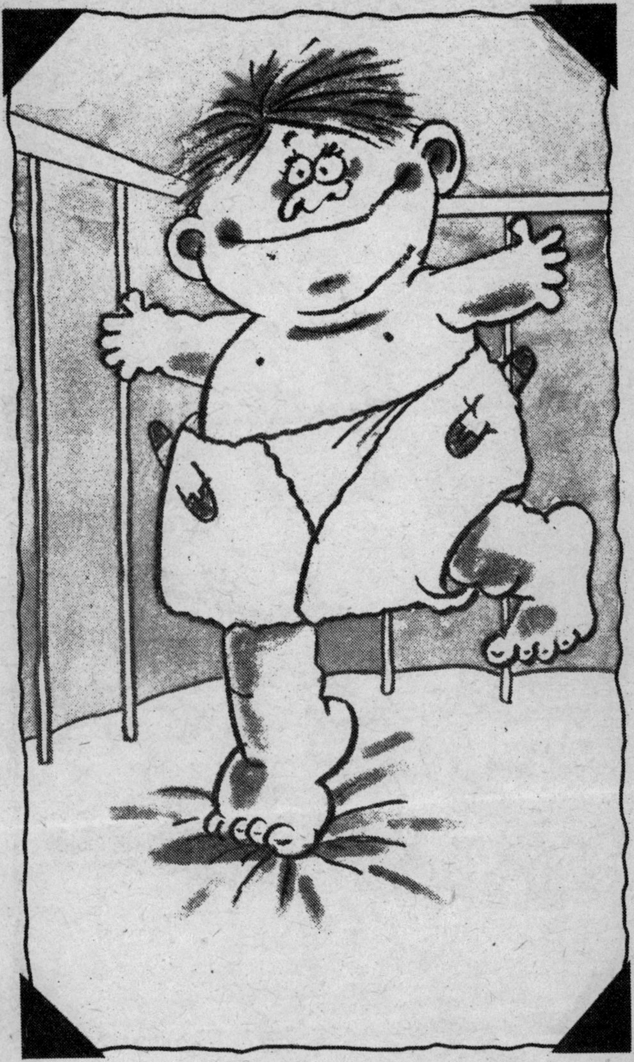

Rudolph Nureyev takes his first step

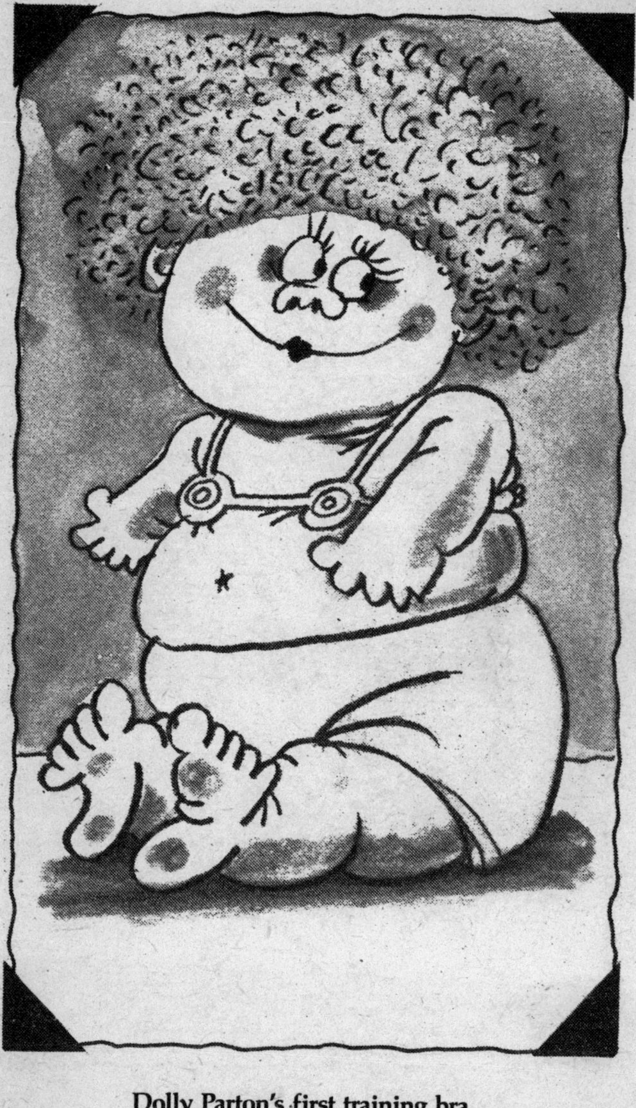

Dolly Parton's first training bra

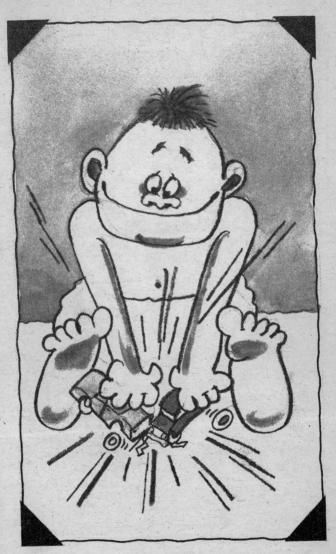

Burt Reynold's with his first toy cars

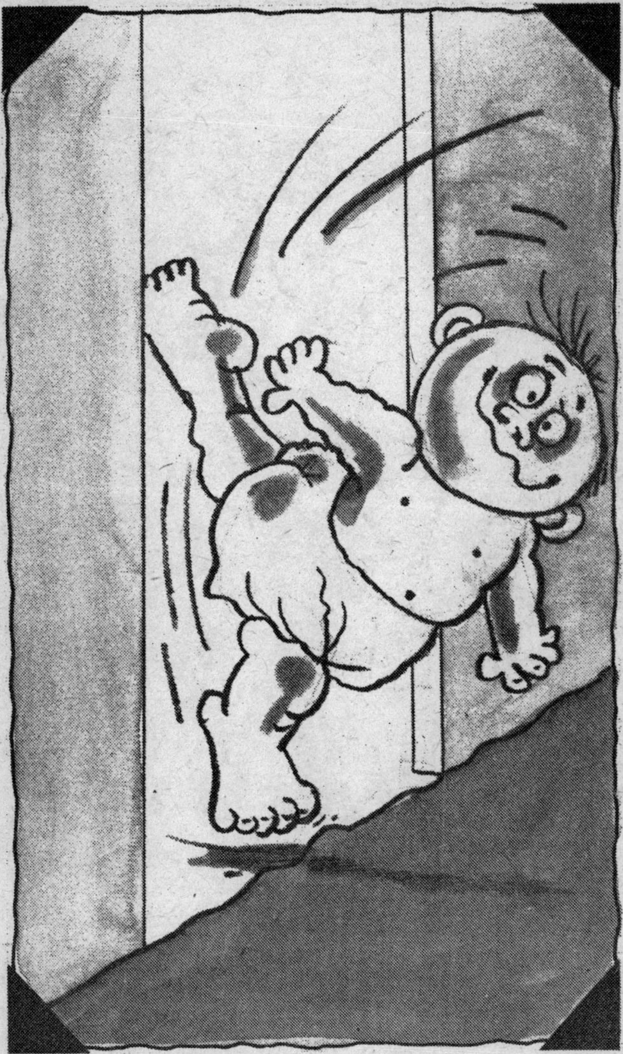

Chevy Chase makes his first entrance

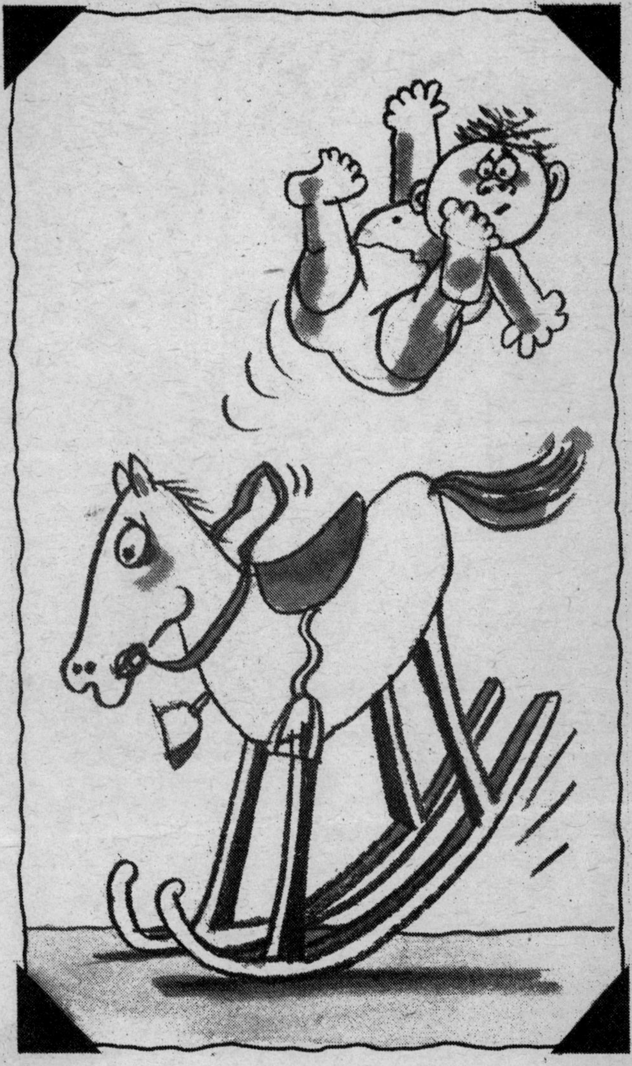

Prince Charles and his first rocking horse

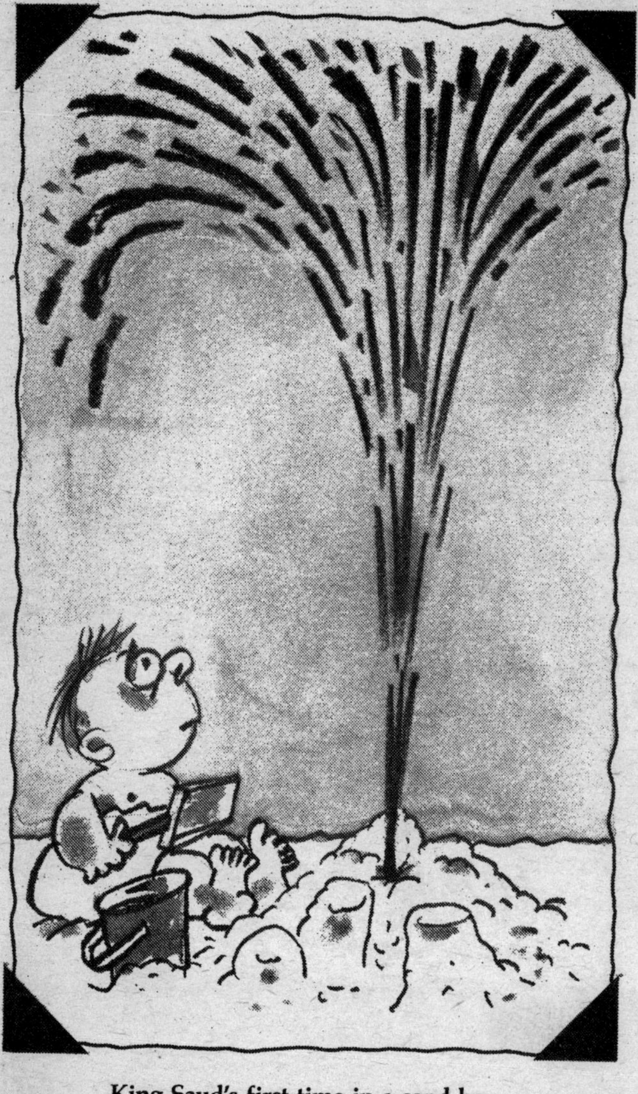

King Saud's first time in a sand box

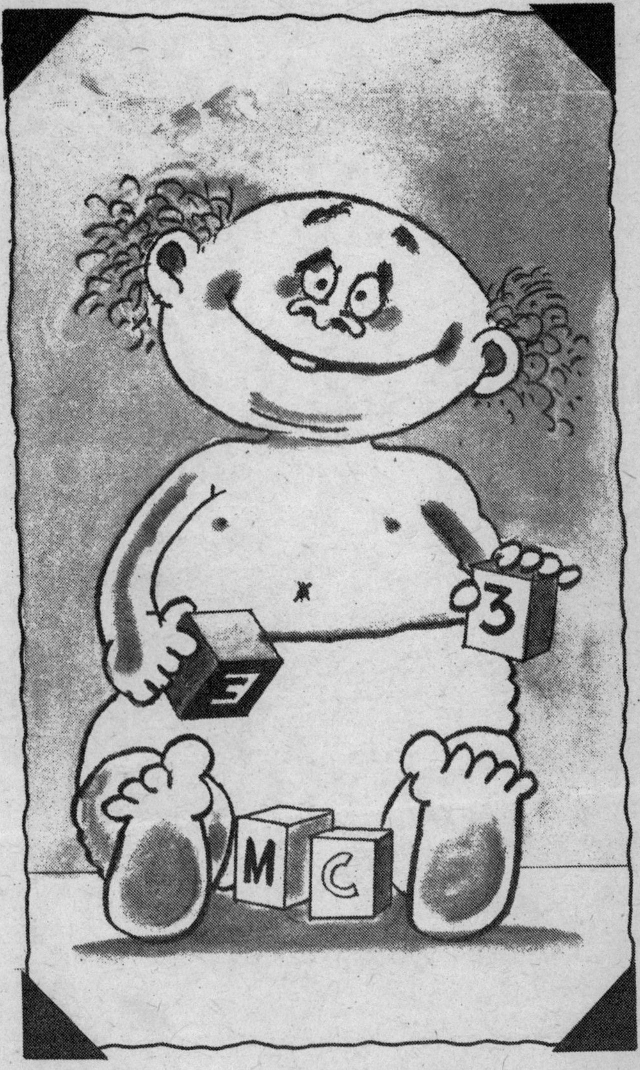
E
3
M
C

Albert Einstein with his first set of building blocks

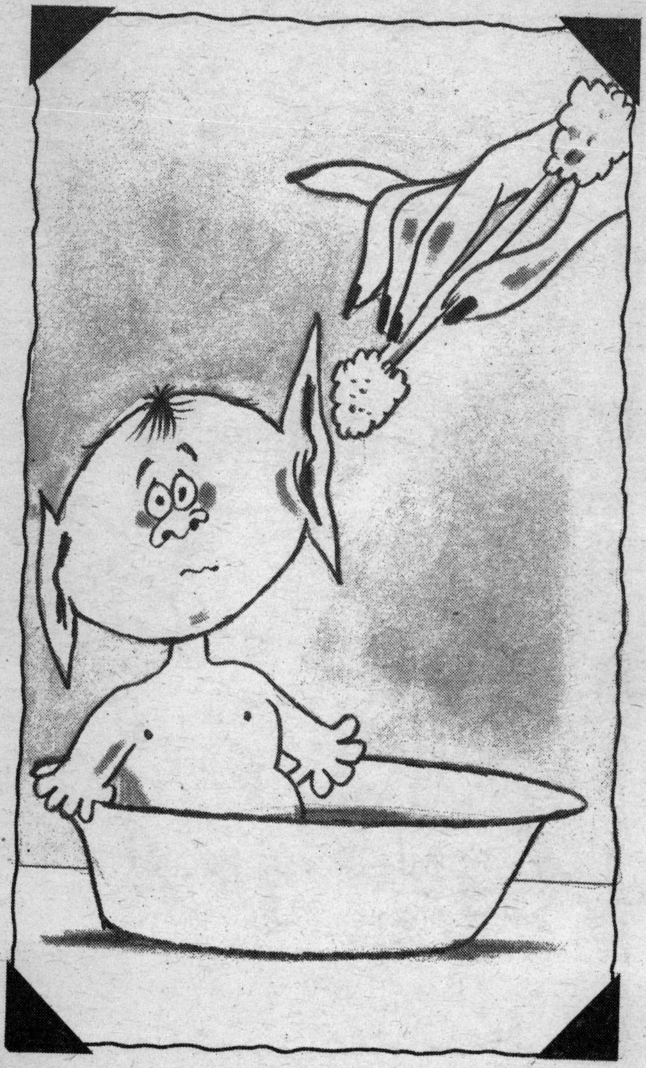

Mr. Spock's first encounter with a Q-tip

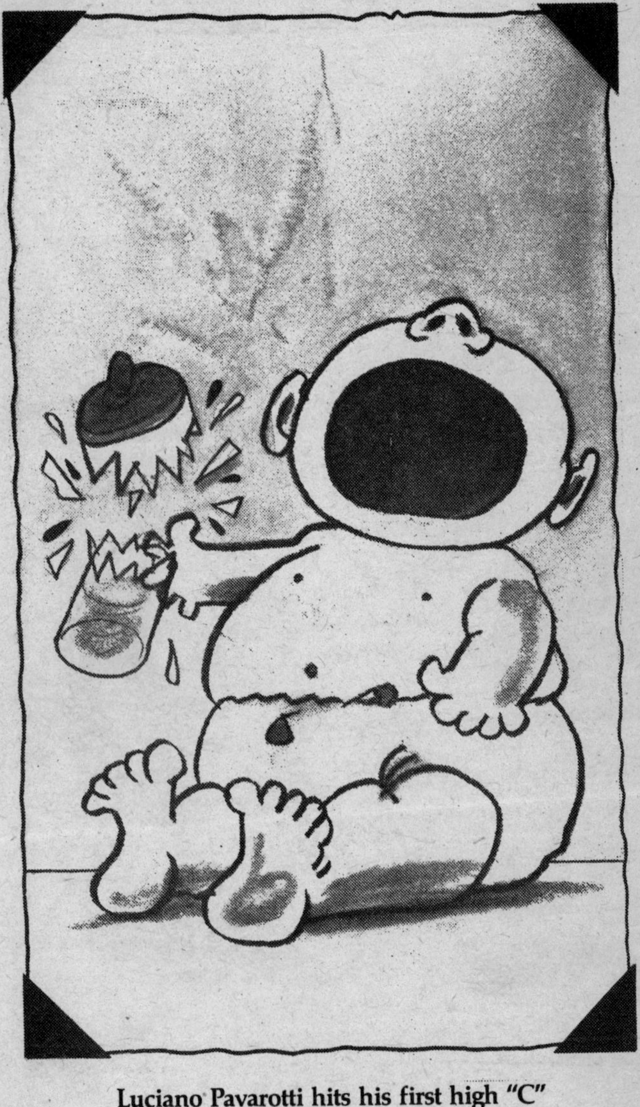

Luciano Pavarotti hits his first high "C"

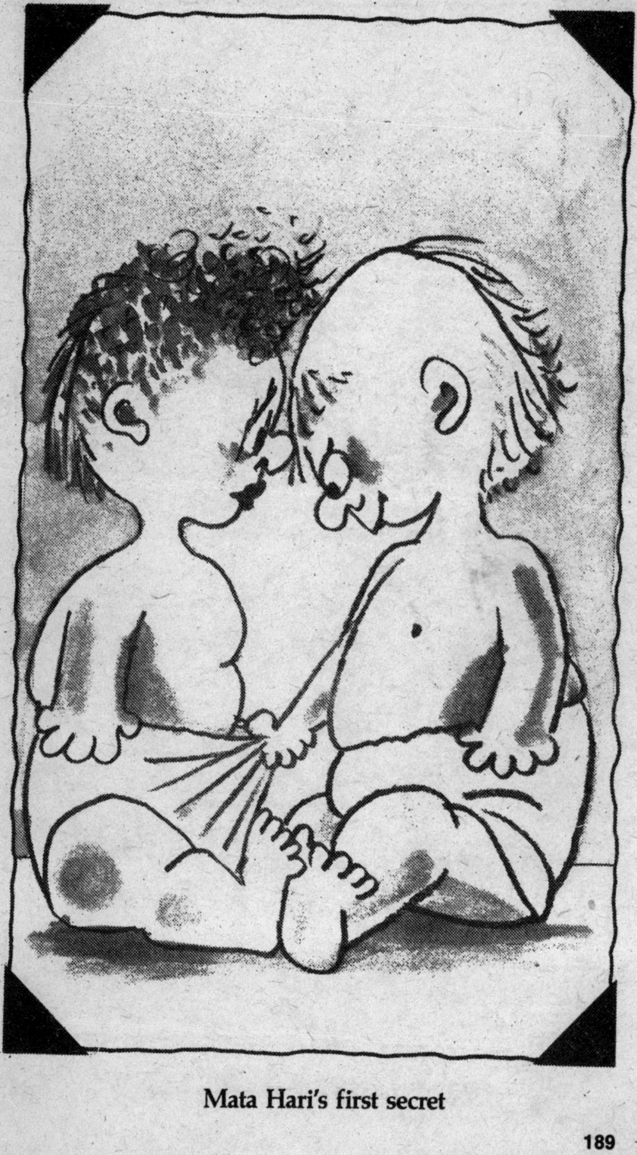

Mata Hari's first secret

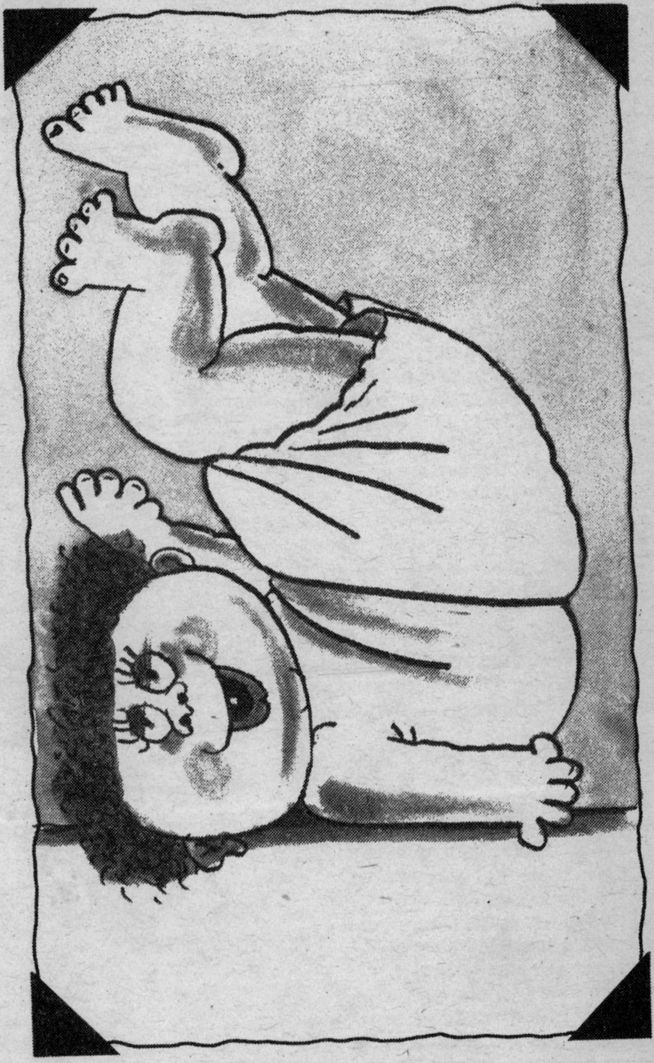

Brooke Shields in her first pose